SCANDALS OF THE POPES

INCLUDING THE PROPHECIES OF SAINT MALACHY

Arthur Crockett, Timothy Green Beckley And Tim R. Swartz

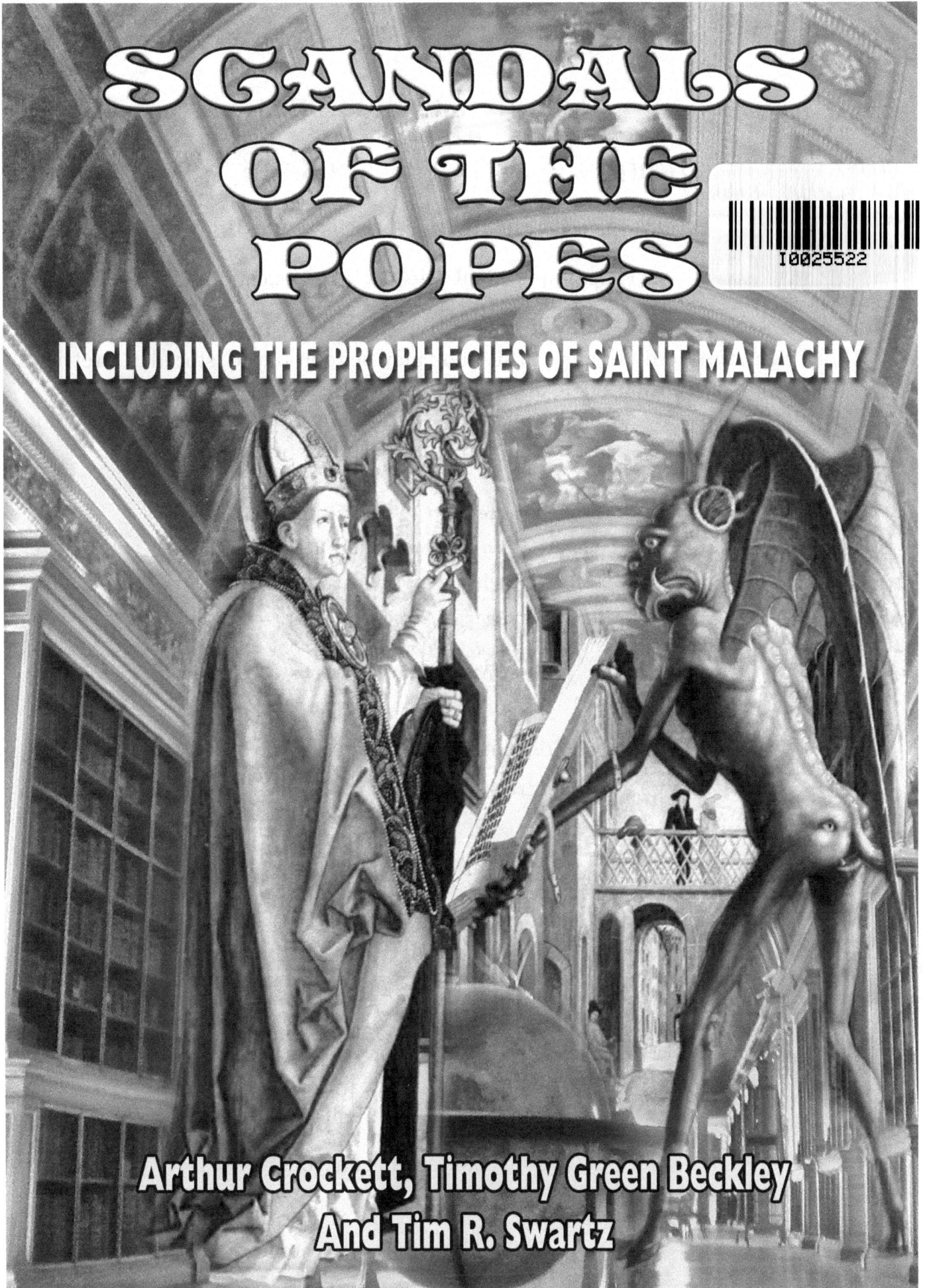

Scandals of the Popes

Including the Prophecies of Saint Malachy

By Arthur Crockett, Timothy Green Beckley and Tim R. Swartz

© 2014 Inner Light/Global Communications

Printed in the United States of America
Timothy Green Beckley: Editorial Director
Carol Ann Rodriguez: Publishers Assistant
Sean Casteel: Associate Editor

Cover Art by Tim R. Swartz

For permission to reprint specific portions or to inquire about foreign rights, address request to: mrufo8@hotmail.com

Free catalog of books upon request:

Global Communications

P.O. Box 753

New Brunswick, NJ 08903

Email: mrufo8@hotmail.com

www.conspiracyjournal.com

CONTENTS

Within the inset illustration:
RECONSTRUCTION OF SHRINE OVER ST. PETER'S TOMB

THE SHRINE IS STANDING AGAINST A WALL OF RED BRICKS

HOLE IN THE RED WALL WHERE THEY FOUND A TINY MARBLE BOX CONTAINING FRAGMENTS OF BONES

ARCH AT THE BOTTOM OF THE RED WALL. REMAINS OF A SKELETON WITHOUT THE HEAD WERE FOUND HERE

ST PETER (THE FIRST POPE) PREACHES THE GOSPEL SHORTLY AFTER THE DEATH OF JESUS. (INSET) SHRINE BUILT OVER THE TOMB OF ST. PETER IN THE VATICAN.

INTRODUCTION:
WITH GOD ALL THINGS ARE POSSIBLE!

Every week the faithful flock to churches around the world to pray and seek guidance. To many it is a fruitless task with no real belief that the supernatural exists, or if it does, that it is possible God could have some positive effect on their lives. To the vast majority, going to church is a chore or a duty—something that is expected of them. They fail to realize that their religion is a living, breathing, entity that is more alive today than it has ever been before.

To an extent, the reason for such a rationalization is steeped in church doctrine itself. Many priests and ministers fail to convey the message that the supernatural powers of the Lord are as real now as they were in the times of the Old and New Testaments. God is not some far off bearded "father figure" we can never get to see. Instead, he is as real as you and I, and if we open our heart to Him, He can touch our very soul.

As the book amply illustrates, God works His miracles in many ways. We have only to keep our eyes and minds tuned in to Him in order for Him to come to assist us. The holiest of mystics—the Saints and the Popes—all realized this fact, and thus, were able to communicate with the Lord whenever it proved necessary. Their God has never been an impersonal God—they have always been able to obtain an audience with the creator as desired.

Unfortunately, a great deal of this truth has always been hidden from the general public for fear they would either not know how to handle it, or that they would use this power for wrongful purposes. The records of the church are clear. There is ample documentation which can be had by those who are willing to dig. This book cuts aside the veil of secrecy and reveals the little known mystical details of the lives of the Popes and the Saints; details that should not have been kept secret from those who are truly looking to be spiritually inspired.

Some of the stories you will read in this book are utterly astounding, a few might be scary, while all are totally absorbing. If nothing more, we know that they will enrich your faith and fill you with the realization that with God all things are possible!

Timothy Green Beckley
Publisher

THE GREAT POPES

MYSTERY OF PETER

"Thou are Peter and on this rock will I build my church, and the gates of Hell shall not prevail against it. And I will give unto thee the keys of the Kingdom of Heaven."

Christ gave this command to Peter and it was recorded by St. Matthew in Chapter 16, verse 18 of his gospel. It marks the birth of the papacy and the inception of the prince of the apostles as the first Pope.

Today, few doubts are concerned with the validity of that command. Millions of Catholics the world over view the Pope as the spiritual link between Christ and ourselves. Other Christians generally think of the Pope as a wise and holy man, which he is. He is regarded as a man with his feet planted firmly on the ground, one who is aware of all things worldly and all things beyond the pale.

However, recorded history tells us more than the church is willing to let on, that many Popes were prophetic and mystical, that they held supernatural powers not usually given to mortal man. Admittedly, not every Pope was so blessed, but many of them held powers which were awesome, or were involved in paranormal events so devastating that scribes immediately recorded them.

After Christ died, St. Peter lived in Antioch for a while, then moved to Rome. He was the Christian leader in Rome and was referred to as the Bishop of Rome and the Pope. Between 64 and 67 A.D., Peter was martyred when Nero began his persecution of Christians. Legend has it that Peter was crucified upside down and is said to have died on the same day as St. Paul.

For hundreds of years the big mystery associated with Peter was his burial place. Has it been found?

***

THE MYSTICAL EXPERIENCE OF POPE CLEMENT VIII

Before we talk about Clement's experience we should say a little about the man. He ruled in the Vatican from January 30, 1592 to March 3, 1605. Pope Clement was pious, just, conscientious, peace-loving and something of a mystic. He listened to criticism with an open mind. He was charitable and enjoyed eating with the poor of Rome, often serving them himself.

In 1954 a group of workers had the job of reinforcing the foundations of St. Peter's Cathedral directly under the main altar. They noticed a patch of loose bricks in a wall. During the process of replacing the bricks the wall caved in.

On the other side they saw a dark, forbidding cavity. Pope Clement was told immediately. He and members of his papal court hurried to the mysterious

opening carrying flaming torches. Clement VIII peered into the darkness, somewhat hesitant about entering the area. And in the flickering light he beheld a large golden cross which glowed at him from deep within the cave.

The mystical experience frightened him. He was awed, too, but did not investigate the vision any further. Instead, he returned to his private apartment, where he found a message waiting for him. It informed him that one of his closest friends had just died.

Was it just a coincidence, or a divine warning? Clement VIII decided on the latter. He ordered that the hole be closed up immediately.

The taboo lasted for about 350 years. Who broke it? And what strange things happened when the hole was opened again?

***

POPE PIUS XII AND THE TOMB OF ST. PETER

Pope Pius XII (1939 to 1958) visited the Vatican Grottoes on June 28, 1949. In this underground church he instructed Mgr. Carlo Respighi to try to find St. Peter's Tomb. A few weeks later the workers lifted part of the floor of the Vatican Grottoes and began to probe the darkness. That was when they found, of all things, a statue of Bacchus, the god of wine and sensuous pleasure! That was the exact spot where St. Peter's tomb was supposed to be! Pius XII was not shocked. He told the workers to keep probing, and when they ran out of funds the Pope financed the excavation out of his own pocket.

Eventually, the skeletal remains of St. Peter were found—but *without a head!* Pope Pius XII made the announcement during the Christmas papal radio broadcast of 1950, although he refrained from pointing out that St. Peter had been decapitated!

***

THE VISIONS OF POPE PIUS XII

If anyone looked the part of the Pope, it was Eugene Pacelli, Pius XII's real name. He was tall, thin, erect, had long, well-shaped hands, a bright look to his eyes, a long aquiline nose and thin lips.

Pius XII was a no-nonsense man. He was brusque and straight to the point. Children, however, melted him, as did the common people of Rome. He had a photographic memory and could commit pages of typewritten material to memory and then "read" what he remembered as though the pages were fixed in his brain.

Pope Pius XII had a number of visions. Many of them were officially confirmed. On October 30, 31 and November 1, 1950, Pius XII spent much of the time in the Vatican garden. It was there on those three days that he saw a repetition of the miracle at Fatima.

To refresh your memory, Fatima is a small village in Portugal. On May 13, 1917 the Virgin Mary appeared before three children while they were in the

fields looking for sheep.

According to historical records, the Virgin Mary predicted five events: 1. the premature death of two of the children who saw the vision of Mary, 2. the end of the First World War, 3. the appearance of a mysterious light which was to precede the outbreak of World War II (such a light was seen in the night sky over much of Europe), 4. minor conflicts after the Second World War, and 5. the conversion of Russia.

The two children who died a short time after the visions of the Virgin Mary were Francisco and Jacinta. Spanish flu took them. The third child, Lucia de Santes, became a nun in the closed order of the Carmelite convent in Coimbra.

The last prophecy of the Virgin Mary has never been officially revealed, though its general content is known. The text says in part, "An impious propaganda will spread terror throughout the world, causing wars and the persecution of the church; many good people will suffer martyrdom; the Holy Father will have much to suffer. If my pleas are heeded Russia will be converted and we shall have peace; otherwise many serious errors will spread in the world; many nations will be destroyed and in the end my Immaculate Heart will triumph and humanity will have a period of peace."

The last part of the prophecy was kept in a sealed envelope and locked in the safe of the Bishop of Coimbra. The envelope was opened in 1960 but its contents were kept secret. Pope Pius knew what was in the envelope because Sister Lucia de Santes had told him a long time before.

***

WHAT PIUS XII SAW IN HIS VISION

You will remember that during the vision of the Virgin Mary, with about 70,000 people present, the sun above Fatima began to rotate in the sky with a fireworks effect. It swung down almost to the horizon and then rose again sharply. This is what pius XII saw in his garden. He also saw the Virgin Mary, although it was never released that he actually spoke to her. In 1950 Cardinal Federico Tedeschini officially revealed the news of the Pope's vision.

***

PIUS XII THE FAITH HEALER

Many miracles have been attributed to Pius XII. All of them deal with faith healings and all of them are carefully documented with testimonials and medical certificates. These documents are kept in a special dossier and are held by the Vatican State Secretariat. These documents are important because some day in all likelihood Pius XII will be canonized.

In fact, the document most likely to be brought forth at that time will be the one that proves that the Pope restored the sight of a boy from Turin. Doctors

cannot give a scientific explanation for the phenomenon.

***

PIUS XII'S VISION OF CHRIST

It was 1954. Pius XII was very sick. The situation was so critical that the Pope's Sacrist, the Dutch Mgr. C. Van Lierde, was summoned to give him extreme unction (the last rites).

The Pope sent him away. Why? Because at dawn the day before, Pius XII had a vision of Christ. Jesus appeared at the foot of his bed and told him that his time had not yet come.

Unfortunately, the Pope later made the mistake of telling his experience to a group of Jesuits. They reported it to the Milan magazine Oggi. The story also broke in London. After that, the Vatican was bombarded with requests for a confirmation. At first there were denials and a "no comment." But Oggi had proof that the Pope had told the Jesuits about his vision. The magazine had the actual speech, with corrections penciled in by the Pope himself. The Vatican then had to issue an official confirmation of the story.

Roman wags then made up jokes about the Pope's vision. One joke was that an American news agency demanded to know what Christ was wearing when he stood at the Pope's bed. A frustrated monsignor was reported to have said, "He was wearing tails, white tie and decorations. That's the way you dress when you have an audience with the Pope!"

Another joke involved the Pope's housekeeper, Mother Pasqualina. She allegedly knocked on the Pope's bedroom door and asked him if he wanted coffee. A powerful voice replied, "Yes, and make it for two!"

***

POPE JOHN XXII—THE MAGICIAN

Pope John XXII whose real name was Jacques Dueze, was a Frenchman whose papacy continued from August 7, 1316 to December 4, 1334. Orthodox biographers deny it but it is well established that John was considered an adept by the alchemists of the day.

Alchemy, of course, was the chemistry of the Middle Ages and dealt with the transmutation of base metals into gold. The biographers were never able to disprove the charge that Pope John held the power to change metal into gold.

John was the son of a cobbler from Cahors. He became a Bishop of Avignon, then a Cardinal. At that time the seat of the Catholic Church was in France, not Rome, and the great poet Dante warned the Italian cardinals to elect an Italian Pope so that the papacy would no longer be subjugated to France.

Nevertheless, John reigned despite much opposition from many quarters and was considered tolerant of his enemies. That is, except one. The man was

Geraud, Bishop of Cahors. History does not make clear why John suspected Geraud, but it is recorded that John was certain the Bishop meant to poison him and the entire college of Cardinals.

The most incredible part of the story is that Geraud was charged with contriving sorceries and diabolical enchantments against John and his cardinals. It might seem inconceivable that the Pope, who was a notable intellect, would believe in black magic. Apparently, he did. Otherwise he would have shrugged off the Bishop's efforts.

What we do have to remember, however, is that we are dealing with the Middle Ages, when the "black arts" had an enormous following. Many people turned to the devil for guidance. There were a great many occult sects roaming Europe, preaching, begging, interrupting church services and scorning monks and priests.

Pope John was thoroughly disgusted with these sects and with magicians who only pretended to be magicians. In the 1320's he issued a series of Bulls equating sorcerers with heretics and authorized punishment for them since they had made a pact with satan. Their books of magic were confiscated and burned.

One of his Bulls dealt with pretended alchemists, whom he condemned because they were charlatans who could not fulfill their promises.

Yet, strangely, Pope John XXII had his own laboratory in Avignon. Did he use it to indulge in alchemy? We know that he was a writer on medical subjects. His Thesaurus Pauperum is a collection of recipes printed in Lyons in 1525 and he authored a treatise on diseases of the eye. He wrote another on the formation of the fetus.

You can be your own judge, remembering that he was a poor man all of his life. Upon his passing, however, it seemed he had suddenly gained greater wealth. When Pope John XXII died his treasure consisted of 200 ingots. Alchemists insist that he manufactured them on one single occasion. One biographer insists this precious metal was worth 660,000 British pounds sterling.

John's coffers also included 18 million florins in gold and seven million in jewels, and there were many valuable consecrated vessels as well. Did he amass such a vast fortune in his laboratory? Alchemsits of the day insist that he did. If he didn't where then did he get it? He conquered no lands, imposed no fines, did not steal from the Church. As the son of a cobbler he never had any real money in his life until he opened his laboratory.

What we do know about Pope John is that he wrote an extensive treatise on alchemy titled "The Elixir of the Philosophers, or the Transmutatory Art of Metals." It was translated from the Latin into French and published in Lyons in 1557, long after Pope John's death. In the treatise he wrote that the

perfect medicine was a combination of vinegar, salt, urine, and sal ammoniac.

Strangely, he added one more ingredient which was never described: sulphur vive.

Pope John XXII may not have been easy on the magicians who roamed Europe during the Middle Ages, but it is apparent that he did believe in the magic of alchemy—and all clues indicate that he had mastered the art of changing base metal into gold.

***

ST. THOMAS AQUINAS—ALCHEMIST

Oddly enough, it was Pope John XXII who canonized Thomas Aquinas in 1323. Oddly, because Aquinas himself was alleged to have been an exceedingly excellent alchemist. The saint was one of the greatest scholars of his age. He was educated by monks at Monte Cassino and later at the University of Naples.

Aquinas was only 17 when he joined the Society of Preaching Friars, or Dominicans, wholly against the wishes of his noble family. His mother was furious that her son had taken the vows of poverty. She did everything in her power to make him change his mind, but to no avail. The Friars shielded him from her appeals by shipping him off to various cities in Italy. He wound up in Rome. His mother followed him everywhere, but was never permitted to see him.

During one low point in his career he was captured by his two older brothers while he was on his way to Paris. Aquinas had hoped to complete his education there. Instead, his brothers locked him up in the castle of Aguino, where he was born. His captivity lasted for two years. Finally, he got word to his superiors, and an escape was arranged from a castle window.

Eventually, Aquinas met the great alchemist Albertus Magnus and became a pupil. He learned a lot of secrets, but the most important one was the secret of making gold from base metals.

Apparently, Aquinas was in communication with the spirit world. At least one occasion on record indicates it, and it was not to his pleasure. The story goes that Magnus spent 30 years creating a man made of brass. It stood in Aquinas' study and one day Aquinas broke it to pieces. He later explained, "I smashed it because the image would not cease talking to me. It interrupted my studies."

There is also evidence that Aquinas delved into magic and became adept at it. He used it once when he learned to his dismay that he had erected his laboratory in the wrong place. It was situated in a large thorough fare where grooms exercised their horses. The noise disturbed Aquinas. He built a small brass horse and buried it in the center of the highway. Then he called

on his powers of magic.

The upshot was that right after he buried the brass horse, no real horse would allow itself to be led down the road. Grooms whipped their horses. They spurred them, coaxed them and even tried to push them. But the horses would not use the road again. In the end, St. Thomas Aquinas had the road to himself, and it was quiet again.

***

POPE PIUS IX—CLAIRVOYANT

Pius IX occupied the "Throne of St. Peter" from 1846 to 1878. His real name was Giovanni Maria, Count Mastai-Ferretti. At his beatification and canonization in Rome 1928, everyone was excited about his remarkable powers of prophecy and clairvoyance.

As you know, much documentation is necessary before anyone achieves sainthood in the Catholic Church. The research may continue for hundreds of years. The Church never hurries such things, saying in defense of itself that it is eternal and that there is never a need for haste.

In the case of Pope Pius IX, the research was begun by Cardinal Cani and then continued by His Eminence Cardinal Ragonesi. He collected an enormous quantity of documentation, which he presented to the Congregation of Rites, all of it dealing with the unique powers of Pius IX.

One of his prophecies dealt with his successor. He told Cardinal Picci on several occasions that he would be Pope when he died. Pius IX was right. Cardinal Picci was elected to Pope on February 20, 1878 and took the name Leo XIII.

Another prophecy by Pope Pius IX was World War I. In 1863 he wrote a letter to the Bishop of Vigevano, saying:

"There will one day be a terrible conflict among men. The good and the evil will pitilessly destroy each other in a monstrous cataclysm, but when the tempest of the human sea has become calm again the barque of St. Peter's will be seen continuing its voyage in full security, more beautiful than ever. For what now constitutes great navies and many kingdoms and republics will become no more than an accumulation of formless debris, only good at best for being cast into the fire."

Rome is really the place to hear all the stories about Pope Pius IX's amazing powers. They still talk about them.

One dramatic event took place during a religious ceremony held in the Pope's private chapel. A large candle stood before a statue of the Madonna. The celebration continued solemnly until someone lighted the candle.

A strange expression crossed the Pope's face as he stared at the flame. Suddenly, he rose to his feet and ordered that the candle be extinguished immediately.

The command was carried out, but no one in the room could understand the reason for it. After the ceremony was over, the candle was examined. In fact, it was taken apart, and found near the top of it was an explosive charge which, if allowed to detonate, would have destroyed many lives.

One day a woman walked into the pontificial ante-chamber and presented her credentials to the Chamberlain. She solicited an audience with Pope Pius IX. She said she was here on a most urgent matter. The Pope was immediately informed, but his reply shocked the Chamberlain. He said, "No, I do not speak with the dead!"

The Chamberlain pressed on, assuming that Pius IX did not quite understand the request. Again the Pope said, "No, I do not speak with the dead!"

When the Chamberlain returned to the ante-chamber he learned that in his absence the woman had dropped dead from a heart attack.

The real shocker, however, was that an investigation showed the woman to be an assassin, and that her mission was to kill the Pope!

To become a saint, it must be proved that the candidate has performed four miracles, two before beatification and two before canonization. Undoubtedly, Pius IX had many miracles attributed to him. We record two here which were quite startling.

At one time two ladies were admitted into the presence of Pius IX. They told him about a deaf and dumb child and begged him to give his blessing to heal the boy. Pius IX replied, "Why ask me for this favor? The child is already cured."

The ladies left the Pope and later found the boy in an animated discussion with an attendant. He was perfectly healthy!

Princess Odescalchi was very ill and was not expected to live. She sent a request to the Pope, asking him for his benediction "in articulo mortis." Pius IX complied, but also sent a message to the princess, saying that "he saw she was not near death and would live for many years."

The woman made a miraculous recovery. She was strong enough a few days later to present herself at the Vatican and was received by Pope Pius IX.

***

POPE PIUS X—ASTROLOGER

Leo XIII once had a private audience with a famed astrologer. It was done at the request of Prince Marco di Colonna. During the interview, Leo XIII sent for Cardinal Sarto, whose first name was Giuseppe.

Cardinal Sarto was deeply interested in numbers and was a student of astrology. The visiting astrologer and Cardinal Sarto hit it off right away.

They had many meetings. The astrologer worked out Cardinal Sarto's horoscope and told the holy man that within three years of their meeting which took place in December 1900, that he would be Pope. Cardinal Sarto replied, "If such is God's will, so be it."

The astrologer was right. Cardinal Sarto became Pope Pius X on August 8, 1903.

The astrologer wanted to know why he chose Pius X as his name. The Pope replied that the number nine had played a most important part in his life. He explained that he was at school at St. Riese for nine years. He was a religious student at Padna for nine years. He was a senate at Tombolo for nine years, a priest at Salzano for nine years, a canon at Treviso for nine years, a bishop at Mantua for nine years, and the Cardinal-Patriarch of Venice for nine years.

The astrologer later guessed that Pius X chose the number ten for an occult reason, or that he may have wanted to break the order of nine that had played so important a role in his life.

It is also interesting to note that for hundreds of years beginning from A.D. 769, the Sacred College of Cardnials, which elects Popes, consisted of only seven cardinals. That mystic number ruled the Conclave for centuries. Eventually it was changed to the number twelve in accordance with the law of the Zodiac, represented by its twelve Houses.

***

THE VISION OF LIBERIUS

Liberius held the "Throne of St. Peter" from May 17, 352 to September 24, 366. Soon after he achieved the papacy he laid the foundations of the arch-basilica of Santa Maria Maggiore, which, as the Basilica Liberiana, became the central church of the Virgin Mary of the Western Church.

Legend tells us that Liberius was commanded by the Virgin Mary in a dream to build a basilica on the spot where he would find snow on August 5th. Because of this, the basilica was known as Santa Maria ad Nives.

***

POPE PIUS X

LEVITATION AND TELEPORTATION

Despite the force of gravity, the human body and almost any inanimate object can be raised from the ground and remain suspended in mid-air without props or without employing a magician's illusion.

The phenomenon is called levitation. It is most closely associated with saints, mystics and people who experience a religious rapture. Levitation is not a rare experience. Most often the power behind it is the result of a good spiritual nature. However, a malignant spirit can also levitate a person, and does so quite often when the person involved is possessed.

Sulpitius Severus described a case of demonic levitation that occurred when St. Martin approached a person possessed by an evil spirit. Severus wrote that "the demoniac raised from the earth and remained suspended in the air, with his arms outstretched, without touching the ground with his feet...You could see the wretched person whirled about in different ways: uplifted and floated in the air with feet upwards, neither did clothes hang down on the face or uncover their bodies in any immodest way."

You can find examples of levitation in the Life of St. Geneviere and the Life of St. Vincent Ferrer. Both books describe how demoniacs who were brought to their presence immediately lifted off the ground. In some cases the demoniacs flew about as birds.

In another official report found in the Bibliotheque Nationale of Paris you can read the amazing story of Francoise Fontaine, a possessed girl who lived in Louviers in 1591. The report says: "And having entered the court—the door of which is under the porch and in the passage of the prison—the girl, Francoise, walked but six paces into the court, and we together with our clerk entered the office where the judge's chair is and the sitting is held, and, as our clerk was beginning to write the present report that we were dictating to him, he cried out and showed us Francoise, who was near the door of the said court, whom we all saw raised about two feet off the floor, upright. At once she fell down on the ground, flat on her back, along the court, with her arms spread out crosswise. Afterwards she was dragged, with her head foremost, still on her back, along the court, without anybody touching her or standing near her, as witnessed the said La Prime, gaoler, the said Nicolas Pellet, servant of the said gaoler, his wife and several prisoners who came into the court, a thing which amazed us much."

At this point the Provost made an attempt to exorcise the possessed girl. He read the Gospel of St. John to her. She was on her back on the floor when he started reading, but then she suddenly raised up to a height of about three or four feet. She was then propelled horizontally toward the Provost. The man was so terrified that he ran into his office.

The report continues:...."As we continued to read the Gospel of St. John, the body of Francoise, who was then lying on the ground, with her face upwards and her arms stretched out crosswise, began to crawl along, head foremost, all disheveled and bristly. All at once, the body of Francoise was raised off the floor, three or four feet high, and borne horizontally, face upwards, along the court, without anything to support her. When we saw her body making straight for us, thus suspended in mid-air, it threw us into such a fright that we withdrew into the office of the court, locking the door behind us and reading the Gospel of St. John down to the end. But the body kept following us through the air up to the office, against the door of which it struck with the soles of its feet, and then was carried back through the air, with the face upwards and head foremost, out of the court. This gave such a fright to the gaoler, her servants, our archers and many prisoners who were present with several inhabitants of Louviers, that they fled, some into the prison, some into the street, after shutting the doors behind them; and the body of said Francoise was carried away out of the court and remained in the passage of the prison, between the door of it and the street-door which the fugitives had shut in their flight. We considered this with great astonishment, till one Desjardins and other prisoners opened the door of the prison and said they would help us, which enabled us to get out of the office and court, having thus found Francoise lying on the ground, close to the prison door."

After some time had passed, Pellet had the idea of giving Francoise the Sacrament. It was not a good move to make. Obviously, Pellet did not realize that the girl was possessed by a demon, and the very last thing the demon wanted her to have was the Sacrament.

The official report states: "...And Francois was raised again several times and even carried away with her head downwards through the church, without being able to take the Sacrament, opening her mouth, rolling her eyes in her head in such a horrible way that it had been necessary, with the help of five or six persons, to pull her down by her dress as she was raised in the air, and they had thrown her down to the floor. Then Pellet had presented the Holy Host again to Francoise, who had knelt down, but she was again snatched off the floor, higher than the altar, as if she had been taken by the hair, in such a strange way that the bystanders were much amazed, and would never have thought of witnessing so frightful a thing, and they all knelt down and began saying prayers."

Pellet again tried to give her the Sacrament. The report continues: "She had for the third time been prevented from taking it, having been for the third time carried over a large bench that was before the altar where Mass was said. She was lifted up into the air towards where a glass had been

broken, with her head downwards and her feet upwards, without her clothes being upset, through which, before and behind, was belching forth much water and stinking smoke. She was then tormented more frightfully than before...and for some time carried through the air, till at last seven or eight men had taken hold of her and brought her down to the ground."

The experience was certainly frightening to the observers, especially when you consider that the instigator of the levitation was a demon. Still, demons hold no corner on the phenomenon. There were any number of levitating saints, although St. Joseph of Copertino probably holds the record for levitating events. In the acts of his canonization there are more than seventy certified cases of rapture with levitation.

***

ST. JOSEPH THE FLYING PRIEST

St. Joseph was born in the year Queen Elizabeth died. He was a slow learner in school and demonstrated no interest in worldly affairs. He was admitted into the Capuchin Monastery of Martina in 1620, but showed no aptitude in mastering even the simplest of tasks. Despite these drawbacks, St. Joseph was such a good-natured person and so devoted to his God that he was permitted to take his vows and become a priest.

St. Joseph's piety, however, got him into trouble. His fame as a pious priest spread far and wide, so far that he was called before the Inquisition of Naples and accused of performing false miracles. Fortunately, he was acquitted and permitted to return to his priestly career.

Most of his levitations are well documented and were witnessed by simple shepherds, famous and high placed people, officials, and even Pope Urban VIII himself.

One important official who witnessed an ecstatic flight by St. Joseph was the High Admiral of Castile. He was the Spanish Ambassador to the Papal Court. In 1645 he passed through Assisi, his wife at his side. His intention was to meet the famed priest.

The two did meet. Then Joseph was ordered to go into the church to talk to the admiral's wife, which he did. But he was hardly inside the church when he suddenly flew into the air and over the heads of the bystanders. He landed at the foot of the statue of the Immaculate Conception, where he spent some moments in prayer. He then flew back to his former place, his mouth open in a great cry. Joseph then returned to his cell.

The admiral and his wife were utterly amazed at what they saw. Their retinue saw it as well and were stupified. The admiral's wife, in fact, fainted and had to be brought around with smelling salts.

***

ST JOSEPH AND THE MANIAC

St. Joseph did not always fly alone. On several occasions he lifted another person and took him with him on an ecstatic flight in a church.

The first time it happened was when Joseph was in the church of St. Clare at Copertino. Joseph attended the ceremony. He knelt alone in the corner of the church, praying. When the choir suddenly burst forth with, "Come, thou bride of Christ," Joseph felt a rush of ecstatic jubilation. He rushed toward the confessor of the convent, grabbed him by the hand, snatched him off the floor and began whirling him around in mid-air.

On another occasion a maniac was brought into the monastery of Assisi to be cured. The maniac's name was Balthasar Rossi and he was strapped to a chair because he was considered dangerous. Rossi had a habit of attacking people because he thought they were mad.

Joseph walked up to the maniac and ordered someone to remove the straps. This was done. Joseph then told the man to kneel, and placed his hand on the man's head. He said: "Do not fear, Chevalier Balthasar; commend yourself to God and His Holy Mother."

Joseph threw his head back and uttered an ecstatic cry of rapture. At that moment, Joseph raised up off the floor, taking the maniac with him. The saint held Balthasar by the head as both remained aloft for about fifteen minutes. Spectators looked on in wonder. On the floor again, Joseph told the man, "Now, cheer up, Chevalier!" And the maniac was cured.

***

ST. JOSEPH AND THE SURGEON

Near the end of his life, St. Joseph needed surgery on his leg. The surgeon, Francesco Perpaoli, witnessed a strange event and later testified to what he had seen:

"During the last illness of Father Joseph, I had to cauterize his right leg by order of Dr. Giacinto Carosi. Father Joseph was sitting on a chair with his leg laid on my knee. I had already begun cauterizing, when I noticed that Father Joseph was rapt out of his senses; his arms were outspread, his eyes open and lifted to Heaven. His mouth was wide open, his breathing had nearly stopped. I noticed that he was raised about a palm over the said chair, in the same position as before the rapture. I tried to lower his leg down, but I could not; it remained stretched out. A fly had alighted on the ball of his eye; in spite of my repeated efforts, I was unable to drive it away, as it kept flying back to the same place. In order to observe Father Joseph better, I knelt down. The above mentioned doctor was examining him with me. Both of us ascertained and undoubtedly that Father Joseph was rapt in ecstasy and actually suspended in mid-air, as I have already said. He had been a quarter of an hour in this situation, when Father Silvestro Evangelista of the monastery of Osimo came up. He observed the phenomenon for some time,

and commanded Joseph under obedience to come to himself, and called him by name. Joseph then smiled and recovered his senses."

***

WHAT IS RAPTURE? WHAT IS UNION?

The best definition of "rapture" and "union" comes from St. Teresa of Avila. This Saint was the famous reformer of the Carmelite Order. Her testimony explaining the sensations experienced while levitating is much too long to include here, but we can highlight it with the following:

During rapture, the soul does not seem to animate the body. A rapture is absolutely irresistible, whilst union, inasmuch as we were still on our own ground, may be hindered, though that resistance be painful and violent; it is, however, almost always impossible. But rapture, for the most part, is irresistible. It comes, in general, as a shock, quick and sharp, before you can collect your thoughts or help yourself in any way, and you see and feel it as a cloud or a strong eagle rising upwards and carrying you away on its wings.

"I repeat it; you feel and see yourself carried away, you know not wither. For though we feel how delicious it is, yet the weakness of our nature makes us afraid at first, and we require a much more resolute and courageous spirit than in the previous states, in order to risk everything, come what may, and to abandon ourselves into the hands of God, and to go willingly wither we are carried, seeing that we must be carried away, however painful it may be. And so trying is it, that I would very often resist and exert all my strength, particularly at those times when the rapture was coming upon me in public. I did so, too, very often when I was alone, because I was afraid of delusions. Occasionally, I was able by great efforts, to make a slight resistance; but afterwards I was worn out, like a person who had been contending with a strong giant; at other times it was impossible to resist at all: my soul was carried away, and almost always my head with it—and now and then the whole body as well, so that it was lifted up from the ground.

"This has not happened to me often: once, however, it took place when we were all together in Choir, and I, on my knees, on the point of commencing to communicate. It was a very sore distress to me; for I thought it was a most extraordinary thing, and was afraid it would occasion much talk; so I commanded the nuns—for it happened after I was made Prioress—never to speak of it. But at other times, the moment that I felt that our Lord was about to repeat the act, and once, in particular, during a sermon—it was the feast of our house, and some great ladies being present—I threw myself on the ground; then the nuns came around to hold me; but still the rapture was observed.

"I made many supplications to our Lord, that he would be pleased to give

me no more of those graces that were outwardly visible; for I was weary of living under such a great restraint, and because his Majesty could not bestow such graces on me without their becoming known. It seems that, in his goodness, he has been pleased to hear my prayer; for I have never been enraptured since. It is true that it was not long ago.

"It seems to me, when I tried to make some resistance, as if a great force beneath my feet lifted me up. I know of nothing with which to compare it; for it is a great struggle, and of little use, whenever our Lord so wills it. There is no power against His power.

"I confess that it threw me into great fear, very great indeed at first, for when I saw my body lifted up from the earth, how could I help it? Though the spirit draws it upwards after itself, and that with great sweetness, if unresisted, the senses are not lost; at least, I was so much myself as to be able to see that I was being lifted up.

"When the rapture was over, my body seemed frequently to be buoyant, as if all weight had departed from it; so much so that now and then I scarcely knew that my feet touched the ground."

***

ST. TERESA'S LEVITATION WITH ST. JOHN OF THE CROSS

The startling event occurred one day when St. John of the Cross visited St. Teresa. They sat in a room which might be described as a parlor or living room. They talked about the Trinity. Suddenly, it became obvious that St. John was rapt in ecstasy. He rose off the floor—chair and all! Seconds later, St. Teresa, who was kneeling, also rose up above the floor.

At that point Sister Beatrice of Jesus entered the room. She witnessed the unusual sight. Later, it was said that a painting of the event was done and the canvas was hung in the room where the double levitation had taken place.

At another time, Sister Anne of the Incarnation was an eyewitness to St. Teresa's levitation. Sister Anne remained mum for about thirty years after the Saint's death. The probability is that she would never have said anything about it if there had been no inquiry. But she was asked to testify at Segovia, and this, in part is what she said:

"On another occasion, between one and two o'clock in the daytime, I was in the choir waiting for the bell to ring, when our Holy Mother entered and knelt down for perhaps the half of a quarter of an hour. As I was looking on, she was raised up about a half a yard from the ground without her feet touching it. At this I was terrified, and she, for her part, was trembling all over. So I moved to where she was, and I put my hands under her feet, over which I remained weeping for something like half an hour while the ecstasy lasted. Then suddenly she sank down and rested on her feet, and turning her head round to me, she asked me who I was, and ordered me under obedience

to say nothing of what I had seen, I said nothing until the present moment."

***

THE TELEPORTATION OF SISTER MARY

Several times the Bible mentions the instantaneous transference of people from one place to another. This phenomenon is called teleportation and holds true for objects as well as people.

If you read the "Acts of the Apostles" you will see that St. Peter, the first Pope, was teleported from Herod's prison. There is also the extraordinary event of the baptism of the Ethiopian by St. Phillip: "And when they were come up out of the water, the spirit of the Lord caught away Phillip that the eunuch saw him no more...But Phillip was found at Azotus." The distance from Gaza, where the baptism took place, to Azotus, is 30 miles.

The Old Testament prophets experienced teleportation, too. Elisha saw Elijah carried away in a whirlwind. Habakkuk was lifted from Judea to Babylon to give food to Daniel in the lion's den.

Sister Mary of Agreda, Spain, was said to have made some 500 teleportation trips between 1620 and 1631. Her instantaneous voyages were all to the same place—the Jumano Indian tribe in New Mexico. During her time spent with the Indians she converted them to Christianity.

The Church didn't know of her teleportations until an official missionary went to New Mexico to tell the Jumanos about Christ. He was shocked to learn that they already knew about Him. The Indians told the missionary that they had been taught by a European nun who wore a blue gown. They showed him things that she had given them, including a chalice with which to celebrate Mass.

The official reported what he had learned to his superiors and an investigation was started. One of the things that was brought out was that the chalice was one from Sister Mary's convent at Agreda.

***

THE TELEPORTATION OF ST. ANTHONY

The Roman Catholic Church does not embrace the subject of teleportation, or being in two places at once, with total acceptance. Its position is ambivalent.

Legend has it that St. Anthony of Padua was preaching in a church in Limoges in 1226 when he suddenly realized that he was supposed to be in another church at the same time. The other church was on the other side of the town.

St. Anthony stopped his sermon, pulled his hood over his head and knelt silently for five minutes. At that exact same period the saint suddenly appeared before the congregation at the other church. He read a passage from the Scriptures and then suddenly disappeared. The hooded, kneeling figure in Limoges then stood and continued speaking.

THE TELEPORTATION OF PADRE PIO

Padre Pio was a Capuchin monk, a miracle worker, a clairvoyant and had the ability to teleport himself at will. He lived from 1887 to 1968 and was a stigmatic. He bled a teacup full every day of his life. His Christ-like wounds have never been accepted by the Church as being from a divine power, but he does have many miracles attributed to him. If the Church ever decides to make him a saint, it won't suffer from lack of documentation.

It has been recorded that Padre Pio restored the sight of a blind girl who had no pupils in her eyes. Records show that he raised the dead and cured incurable cancer. One pilgrim said: "I was there when Padre Pio picked hunchbacks off the floor and straightened their backs. I saw him cure cripples."

Despite the Church's position on Padre Pio's stigmata, it was quite real. The monk had five open wounds that never healed, nor did they ever become infected. His chest wound was in the shape of an inverted cross. When Padre Pio served Mass he always wore gloves with the fingers cut off. He did not want his palms to be seen by the congregation.

There is also testimony that Padre Pio had the ability to seemingly drop in from nowhere. The monk rarely left his monastery near Poggia, Italy, yet he was able to teleport himself when he thought he was needed somewhere.

During World War I, for instance, he suddenly appeared in the tent occupied by a general. The Italian officer was about to take his own life with a gun. The monk pleaded, "Such an act is foolish." The general agreed and put the gun away. He had never seen the Capuchin monk before, but later when he happened to visit the monastery at Poggia, he recognized Padre Pio as the priest who materialized in his tent.

Padre Pio was on hand during World War II. The plane of an Italian pilot was hit during a dogfight. The pilot jumped out and pulled his parachute cord. The parachute did not open. His body hurtled toward the earth. He faced certain death. Then suddenly something or someone caught him in mid-air. He saw that it was a friar. The pilot was carried gently to earth, then the apparition disappeared.

The story did not sit at all well with the commanding officer. He was sure the pilot was in shock, so he sent him home on leave. He told his mother about his strange experience, but she wasn't shocked at all. She simply nodded her head and told him, "Yes, that was Padre Pio. I prayed to him so hard for you."

She showed her pilot-son a picture of the monk. It was the same man who had caught him in mid-air!

The pilot then went to Poggia to thank the priest...and got an even bigger surprise. Padre Pio told him, "That is not the only time I have saved you. At

Monastir, when your plane was hit, I made it glide safely to earth."

This revelation truly astonished the pilot because there was no way Padre Pio could have known about the incident which had happened years earlier!

***

TELEPORTATION OF CHILDREN

Dr. Joseph Lapponi, who was medical officer to Popes Leo XVII and Pius X, wrote a book in 1906 describing the startling appearances and disappearances of the Italian brothers Alfred and Paul Pansini, aged ten and eight.

On one occasion the boys disappeared from their home in Ruvo and appeared at their uncle's home in Trani, miles away. At another time they were in Ruvo's main square when they suddenly wound up on a ship in the ocean. Apparently, the brothers disappeared quite often, ending up in other towns in Italy. The strange event occurred so often that their mother was beside herself with concern. She consulted Bishop Berardi. The holy man went to see for himself. Young Alfred and Paul were placed in a room in which the door and windows were closed and locked. When the bishop walked in, the boys were gone.

The author of the book said that there was no real explanation except that the brothers were being teleported to other places probably against their will.

In another case, three children in San Jose, Costa Rica were teleported during a seance. The year was 1907. When the seance started, the children, aged twelve, ten and seven, were in the room. All the doors and windows were locked. They were teleported into the garden outside.

The same thing happened again and again for the next two years. In 1909, one of the participants suggested that when the children knocked on the door to get back into the house after their teleportation, they should not be let in. Instead, the spirits should be asked to teleport the children back where they had come from.

The experiment was tried. With all doors and windows locked, the children in the garden were told to stay there. Moments later all three reappeared in the room while many witnesses watched in astonishment. Someone asked the children how it felt to be teleported and they replied that it felt like someone was lifting them under their arms and placing them in another area.

***

MADAME SAGE'S REMARKABLE STORY

The year was 1845. The locale was Livonia, Russia. Madame Sage—she was known by no other name—was in an almost continual state of teleportation. According to contemporary reports, the woman was actually in two places at once.

Madame Sage was a teacher in a girls' school. Students reported on many occasions that the woman would sit facing the class while another image of Madame Sage would write lessons on the blackboard. Two pupils insisted they saw her sitting indoors while at the same time she was in the garden picking flowers.

The girls' imaginations could have been over-active, yet an adult was an eyewitness to Madame Sage's strange double image. One day the adult witness visited the teacher when she suffered a cold. Madame Sage was in bed—yet her double roamed the room at the same time!

Eventually, the school governors called the Madame in for an explanation. She admitted to them that she could freely project an image of herself any time she wanted to. It was nothing more than a matter of willpower. She was dismissed from her job and her recorded history stops there.

***

THE HOLY HOUSE AT LORETO

The Holy House is a small stone building, now incorporated into a large basilica. It can be seen at Loreto, near Ancona in central Italy. It is allegedly the home of the Virgin Mary and her family when they lived in Nazareth.

According to legend, on May 10, 1291, this little house in Nazareth was levitated off its foundation and moved to Dalmatia, where it settled on the summit of a hill at Tersatto, a small town about sixty miles from Trieste.

The people of Dalmatia woke that morning to find the house in their midst, and made of reddish stone, with a wooden roof painted blue and decorated with stars. Inside, the curious villagers found earthenware vessels and a small altar with a wooden cross over it. The cross bore the inscription: "Jesus nazarenus rex judaeorum." To the right of the altar was a cedar statue representing the Virgin with a child in her arms.

The village priest had a vision of Mary, who told him: "Know that the house which has been brought of late to your land is the same in which I was born and brought up. Here, at the annunciation of the Archangel Gabriel, I conceived the Creator of all things. Here the word of the eternal Father became man. The altar which was brought with the house was consecrated by Peter, Prince of the Apostles."

After three years and seven months, the house was levitated again and brought to its present location in the hills behind the Marche coast.

***

BILOCATION OF NATUZZA EVOLO

This remarkable woman still lives in the city of Paravati, Italy. She was born in 1924. Natuzza Evolo is married and has five children. She is a Calabrian peasant who has the ability to see the spirits of the dead and can diagnose illnesses.

Since 1974 her powers have been studied by Valerios Marinelli, a professor of engineering at the University of Calabria. So far, he has collected and documented 52 cases in which Natuzza has bilocated, meaning that she has been in two places at the same time.

Marinelli summarizes one of the cases: "In August 1975, Professor Jole Gualtiere was in Sicily. Waking up one morning she found bloodstains on the sheet and on the cushion of her bed. They did not seem to be her stains, as she had no wounds. As she knew that Natuzza had the power of leaving bloodstains, she phoned her husband, engineer Leonardo do Romano, who was in Calabria, and told him: 'Go to Natuzza and ask her to narrate something to you.' Jole did not say anything else, because she wanted to see if her hypothesis—that it had been Natuzza—was correct. When Leonardo arrived at Paravati, Natuzza met him at the door, saying: 'I knew you would come; I have been waiting since this morning. Last night, I visited your wife, in Sicily, and left some bloodstains on the bed, and some fingerprints with which I touched the sheet.' "

**

TELEPORTED 9,000 MILES

The Spanish soldier was on guard duty with other members of his regiment in Manila in the Philippines. It was late at night, October 24, 1593. Suddenly, he found himself standing in the main square of Mexico City, Mexico. At first he really didn't know where he was, but after asking some questions he learned the locale and also learned that it was still October 24.

The Mexican authorities didn't believe him, naturally. It was true that the insignia on his uniform indicated that he was with a Manila garrison, and it was also true that neither the uniform nor the soldier appeared to be travel-worn. Still, he was jailed as a deserter.

The soldier's only hope of vindicating himself was to reveal what had happened back in Manila just before his strange travel experience. He told his captors that the governor of the Philippines, Don Gomez Perez Dasmarinas, had been murdered.

It took weeks for that news to reach Mexico. When it did, the Spanish soldier was accused of witchcraft. He denied the charge. The Inquisitors ordered that he be returned to Manila and face an investigation there. It was then that the soldier was finally exonerated because there were witnesses who claimed that the soldier was definitely on guard duty on the night of October 24.

**

TELEPORTING MEDIUMS

Medium William Eglinton was at a seance in London in 1878 when one of the sitters suggested that Eglinton should be taken through the ceiling. The

response was immediate. The medium disappeared. Then a loud thump was heard from the room above. The sitters hurried upstairs and found Eglinton on the floor above and in a trance.

In another case, medium Carmine Mirabelli stood with friends in a railroad station in Sao Paulo, Brazil. They were there to see Mirabelli safely off on his journey to Sao Vincente, about fifty miles away. Then quite unexpectedly, Mirabelli disappeared.

A quick search was made of the railroad station, but he was not to be found. An astute member of the group decided to call the people Mirabelli was going to see in Sao Vincenti. He learned that medium had arrived two minutes after he was declared missing in Sao Paulo.

In 1928 multiple eyewitnesses saw the teleportation of the Marquess Centirione Scotto, a medium. The group was at Millesimo Castle. During a seance in which the lights were turned off, the sitters heard Scotto say, "I can no longer feel my legs." Then there was silence. Someone spoke to the marquess, but there was no reply. When the lights were turned on, Scotto's chair was empty.

The doors and windows were still locked on the inside. The castle was searched thoroughly, but there was no sign of the missing medium. A psychic in the group said she was going to try to reach her spirit guide through automatic writing. The pencil in her hand began to write: "Do not be anxious. Medium is asleep. Go to the right, then outside. Wall and gate. He is lying—hay—hay—on a soft place."

The group followed the directions and found themselves in a granary in the stable yard. The door was locked. Someone went for a key. The door was then opened. But inside the building there was another door, and that, too, was locked. The key dangled on the outside of the door. When this door was unlocked the group found Scotto sound asleep on a pile of hay.

There were ten witnesses to this phenomenon. Their report on the story was later published in an Italian magazine called Luce e Ombra.

TELEPORTATION OF MAJOR POOLE

Major Wellesley Tudor Poole published a volume of memoirs in 1962. Major Poole had a distinguished military career, and his book, The Silent Road, tells of an extraordinary experience he had on a stormy December night in 1952.

He was stationed at a country station in Sussex, England, about a mile and a half from his home. It was 5:55 p.m. There were no cabs and it was raining hard. He was desperate to get home by six o'clock because he expected an overseas call at that time. he tried to telephone home, but the station's public phone booth was out of order.

He wrote in his book: "In despair I sat down in the waiting room and

having nothing better to do, I compared my watch with the station clock. Allowing for the fact that the exact time was 5:57 p.m., I had three minutes to zero hour! What happened next I can't say. When I came to myself I was standing in my hall at home, a good 20 minutes' walk away, and the clock was striking six. My telephone call duly came through a few minutes later. Having finished my call, I woke to the realization that something very strange had happened. Then much to my surprise, I found that my shoes were dry and free from mud, and that my clothes showed no sign of damp or damage."

* * *

UFOs LINKED TO TELEPORTATIONS

Much has been written about an event which took place on November 9, 1973 in New York State. Uri Geller, the Israeli psychic, said that he was teleported from New York City to Ossining, some 150 miles away. He wound up in the home of psychical investigator Andrija Puharich. There were witnesses to the event. Both participants claimed at the time that they were in contact with space beings and that they had seen several UFOs.

In an even more famous case, Betty and Barney Hill were motoring back from Canada to their home in New Hampshire when they saw a strange object in the sky. As it neared the couple they were able to distinguish beings looking at them through windows. The Hills made an effort to get away from the object, but both fell unconscious at the same time. When they came to two hours later they were 35 miles nearer to their home.

Betty and Barney had no recollection of what happened during those two hours. Each was hypnotized later, and each recalled the same series of events, which included being taken aboard a UFO and undergoing a medical examination. Neither participant could remember driving those 35 miles, even under hypnosis!

In this case there were no eyewitnesses. Betty and Barney Hill were on the highway alone. No one saw them teleported to the space ship. Other recent events, however, lead us to wonder if UFOs might have been responsible for the teleportations of the ancient prophets. Some scholars believe that angels and UFOs are related, that these craft could be of "heavenly origin." Did St. Peter use a UFO? Did Sister Mary make her 500 trips across the ocean on a UFO? And how about Padre Pio? He had appeared in mid-air to catch a falling pilot. UFOs have the ability to hover in flight. We are suggesting that divine power played a part in these teleportations, and that UFOs are divinely inspired. Even Billy Graham says this may be the case. By way of argument, examine the following cases.

The year was 1959. A well-known businessman in Bahia Blanca left a hotel in that city and got into his car. After he started his engine the car

suddenly appeared to be enveloped in a dark cloud. Before he knew it he was standing next to a road on an unfamiliar countryside.

He hitched a ride on a truck and asked the driver if he would take him to Bahia Blanca. The driver told him it was not possible. They were in Salta, 620 miles from Bahia Blanca.

The businessman got out of the truck near a local police station and persuaded the officers to let him call the police in his home town. He was afraid that he had suffered amnesia and that a huge chunk of his life was gone forever. Instead, a few minutes later he heard a scary truth. The police in Bahia Blanca called back and told him that his car was still parked in front of the hotel and that the engine was still running! Time lapse had been only a few minutes.

What was the mysterious fog that enveloped the man's car? Did it come from a UFO, and was its origin spiritual? No one has been able to give a satisfactory answer to that question, but other cases do exist.

***

STRANGE MIST IN ARGENTINA

Dr. and Mrs. Gerardo Vidal left a family reunion party in Argentina. They drove into a patch of fog or mist and everything went blank. When they finally became aware of their surroundings they found themselves on a road near Mexico City—4500 miles from their starting point. The time lapse here was forty-eight hours. They could not have traveled that distance by any normal means. The doctor called his family in Argentina and told them that neither he nor his wife had any recollection of how they got to Mexico, or what had transpired during the missing 48 hours from their lives. In this case, every member of the party was a circumstantial witness to the strange journey.

***

MYSTERIOUS FOG IN JAPAN

In some of the cases in which a mist envelops an individual, the car he is driving in also disappears. This was the situation in Japan on March 4, 1964. The car had Tokyo license plates. The driver was alone in front. In back, an elderly man read a newspaper. The car was a large black one and it was on a crowded highway.

In this case there were three eyewitnesses to the phenomenon. They were officials of the Fuji bank and were on their way to a golf course. Their car was directly behind the large black one.

One of the witnesses told a Tokyo reporter that "a puff of something gaseous, like white smoke or vapor, gushed out from somewhere around the black car, and when this cloud dispersed (a matter of not more than five seconds), the black car had vanished."

TOP LEFT - POPE PAUL III
BOTTOM LEFT - POPE JULIUS II
TOP RIGHT - POPE EUGENIUS IV
BOTTOM RIGHT - POPE ALEXANDER VII

ALEXANDER VII ... CHISIVS SENEN
PONTIFEX ... MAXIMVS
CREATVS DIE VII ... PRILIS MDCLV

TOP LEFT - POPE CLEMENS XIV
BOTTOM LEFT - POPE LEO X
TOP RIGHT - POPE URBANUS VI
BOTTOM RIGHT - POPE BENEDICTUS XV

THE BOX NO POPE WILL OPEN

The Panacea (Cure-All) Society of Bedford, England has in its possession a strange box which weighs 156 pounds and is sealed with copper nails. It can be opened only when 24 bishops agree to pass judgment on its contents. The last known attempt to bring that about was made on St. George's Day in 1935, when representatives of the Panacea Society brought a petition of 30,000 signatures to Lambert Palace pleading for the box to be opened. The Archbishop of Canterbury at that time refused to honor the petition, saying that he had been unable to review the decision that had been made many years ago.

An official of the Society says: "We can guarantee that it (the box) is ready for production if and when the bishops condenscend to play their part."

On a regular basis the Panacea Society places an advertisement in British newspapers. The wording never varies. It reads: "Crime and Banditry, Distress of Nations and Perplexity will continue to increase until the Bishops open Joanna Southcott's Box of Sealed Writings."

***

WHO WAS JOANNA SOUTHCOTT?

The woman was born in 1750 in a thatched cottage in Gittisham in the English county of Devon. Her parents were poor farmers. Even as a child, Joanna was quite devout. She carefully marked off one section of the family's garden and named it "Gethsemane." Her first experience of feeling God's pure strength flowing through her veins occurred when she was a teenager. She sat at the bedside of a dying man. He sat up suddenly and cried out that the "black dogs of hell" were clawing at the windows for him with "Satan's eyes glowing like coals in the shadows."

Joanna stood up quickly and exorcised the presence of evil, saying: "Satan, I charge thee by the living word of God to go hence and trouble this soul never again."

The dying man dropped back on his pillow. His expression was one of peace. He died shortly before dawn.

Joanna was 42 when she heard a "voice" speak to her. The year was 1792. She had her menopause. Europe was being torn apart by the French Revolution and terrible stories were being brought across the Channel to England. The "voice" said: "The Lord God is awakening out of His sleep. He will shake the earth terribly. There shall be wars and rumors of wars. Nation shall rise against nation, and kingdom against kingdom. There shall be famines and pestilences and earthquakes. The sign of the Son of Man shall appear in Heaven and He shall come in clouds with power and great glory.

A UFO associated with divine intervention? No one knows. It remains one of the mysteries yet to be solved.

* * *

MEDALLION HONORING FLYING SAINTS

Watch, therefore, for ye know not what hour your Lord doth cometh."

Joanna had a premonition about the "voice" coming to her. There were knockings and rappings on her bed, doors and windows. She said, "The words were so dreadful that they made me tremble."

At times, sleep became impossible. There were more tappings and more strange visitations. She was commanded to write down what was said to her, so she did, filling page after page with spiritual messages.

At one point Joanna was told to "make known to the church that these things are of God, even His voice uttering the prophecies of the Latter Day." The woman was hesitant about revealing her visitations until her dead mother came through to her. Joanna asked her by what spirit had all these messages come to her and her mother told her they were from the Lord.

***

JOANNA'S AUTOMATIC WRITING

With no more doubt in Joanna Southcott's mind, she settled down to write of her experience. But she learned that her writing hand was under someone else's control, that she merely held her pen poised. The phenomenon is known as automatic writing. And according to Joanna, the "voice" now used her pen as though she was merely a secretary taking dictation.

The handwriting itself was an angular scrawl and barely legible. Some of the messages were jingles and some were sort of sing-song rhyming prose which went on and on.

***

JOANNA FAILS TO INTEREST THE CHURCH

The woman's effort was to convince the Methodists and Dissenters that her messages were from God. They turned her away. She then visited the Rev. Joseph Pomeroy, vicar of St. Kew in Cornwall. He represented the Church of England. He showed some interest, but made no commitment. In 1796 Rev. Pomeroy went to see Joanna's employer (Joanna was a domestic). He wanted to make an investigation. Instead, he was confronted by Joanna, who read him some passages from her writings. He told her it sounded like the Devil's work. Then he told her employer that she would soon be out of her mind.

Nevertheless, Pomeroy was concerned. He made another visit three months later and attempted to stop Joanna's predictions. But she was adamant. The reverend then suggested to her that she permit a jury of clergymen to examine her writings and then abide by their decision. The woman agreed.

Before he left she handed him a sealed envelope and asked him not to open it until Christmas. Rev. Pomeroy did as he was asked. On Christmas he opened the envelope and read the message. It said that the Bishop of Exeter,

who was in good health, would not live to see the holidays. Joanna had been right. The Bishop had died unexpectedly on December 12.

There were other predictions from Joanna that came true, and Rev. Pomeroy was duly impressed. Still, he was not prepared to champion her claims. In 1798 she wrote letters to the Bishop and other dignitaries of the church, demanding that they go to Rev. Pomeroy's rooms to examine the papers she had left there. The move merely provoked the church and nothing was done.

***

JOANNA PUBLISHES HER PAPERS

The woman had saved some money for her old age and used it now to have her messages printed in Exeter. In 1801 her first book appeared. It was a 48-page pamphlet titled "The Strange Effects of Faith." It described her mysterious communcations and her seemingly never-ending fight for recognition. And on the first page of her book she set down her challenge—a challenge that has not yet been met:

"If any 12 ministers who are worthy and good will prove that these writings come from the Devil, I will refrain from further printing. If they cannot, I shall go on."

Eventually, rumors about her strange predictions spread all over England. Rich men wrote to her for more information about herself. She invited them to come to her home to examine her writings. She told them to bring along the Bishop and any other church dignitary they could find. Seven men did come to her home, but they could not persuade any churchmen to accompany them. The Bishop said the woman was mad.

The visitors read much of what Joanna had written and were impressed.

***

JOANNA'S SEALED BOX

The seven men suggested to the woman that she place her writings in a sealed box. Mr. William Sharp, a well-known engraver, was one of the men. He wrote later: "I had a large case made which enclosed the whole box, for the cords around it were sealed with seven seals, and I put tow between the box and the case, that the seals might not be broken.

Joanna wanted the return of the prophecies she had given to Rev. Pomeroy, but in a fit of anger and exasperation he flung them into the fireplace.

Joanna was heartbroken. The papers Rev. Pomeroy burned were important to her. They were the proof that she was a creditable prophet. Her seven sponsors then assuaged her feelings by inviting her to London on an all-expenses-paid trip. And with the help of these men she was able to begin a propaganda assault on Parliament. Joanna had the men write letters to the

Lords Spiritual and Temporal and to the members of the House of Commons. The effort failed to stir interest in her.

But there was a positive side, too. Her followers grew in number. One of them was the owner of a large paper mill. He brought her a ream of paper as a gift. Whether by impulse or divine guidance, Joanna cut the paper into squares and drew a circle on each one. Inside the circles she wrote: "The Sealed of the Lord, the Elect and the Precious, Man's redemption to Inherit the Tree of Life, to be made Heirs of God and Joint Heirs with Jesus Christ."

These slips of paper would be membership cards of her mission to overthrow Satan. Joanna felt that he controlled the world, and it would be reclaimed only when enough of its inhabitants renounced Satan and pleaded for deliverance. When a believer signed the paper it was folded like an envelope and then sealed with Joanna's special seal, bearing the monogram "I.C." (Jesus Christ). The seals were then regarded as the symbols of her campaign.

***

JOANNA'S "TRIALS"

Her sponsors were anxious to put Joanna's claims to a public test. What they wanted was to vindicate her. To do so, they devised a public "trial." Personal invitations were sent to Bishops and other religious officials. On the day of the "trial" however, in January, 1803, only 53 persons showed up. And all of them were believers.

A second trial was arranged for December 5, 1804. This time hundreds of believers arrived, but not one who had to be convinced of Joanna's powers.

***

JOANNA—THE SECOND EVE

At one point in her career, Joanna believed that she was the second Eve. She was convinced that she was the woman who would redeem mankind from its original sin, offsetting what the first Eve had done in the Garden of Eden.

Joanna also found passages in Revelation which referred to her. She was the woman "clothed with the sun," who had the "moon under her feet and upon her head a crown of twelve stars." She was convinced that those who followed her would be among the 144,000 Elect mentioned in Revelation.

***

JOANNA AND THE SECOND MESSIAH

Twenty years after she had her menopause, Joanna heard a voice say: "This year thou shalt bear a son by the Power of the Most High."

She was thrilled. She wrote a book about it and called it the "Third Book of Wonders." Again, Revelation promised the Second Coming and Joanna reminded her readers that the birth of Shiloh, the Second Messiah, would

occur on October 19, 1814. She invited the physicians of many famous people of the day to come to her to verify the miracle pregnancy. The response was overwhelming when 21 doctors showed up. Her pregnancy was confirmed by 17.

When the great day approached, crowds gathered outside her home. Carpenters made an ornate cradle to receive the Messiah. But when the day came, nothing happened. So a new date of December 24 was announced.

But something went wrong. Joanna became ill. December 24 came and went, but there was no baby. The woman's illness worsened. And on December 27, Joanna Southcott died. An autopsy revealed no baby, but her womb was extremely swollen.

According to the orders left by Joanna, the box was not to be opened until 24 bishops agreed to pass judgments on its contents. Strong efforts were made by her followers to see that her orders were carried out. Letters were written to every dignitary in England, including Queen Victoria, but so far all efforts have failed.

***

WHAT THE BIBLE SAYS

If you read Revelation xi 19; iv. 4. 10 you will find the following words:

"And the temple of God was opened...and there was seen the Ark (chest or box) of His Testament (or Will)...And round about the Throne were four-and-twenty Elders (Bishops) sitting...And they fall down and cast their crowns (their wisdom) before the Throne."

Does this refer to Joanna's Box? You be the judge.

* * *

NOTE—

IT WAS NOT JOANNA SOUTHCOTT'S BOX that was opened on the 11th of July 1927.

This is
THE REAL
  BOX,
it weighs 156 lbs., is nailed with copper nails, and is in safe keeping.

ST. MALACHI'S PROPHECY OF THE POPES

One of the most startling sets of prophecies to be found in religious history concerns itself with St. Malachi and the predictions he made for all of the Popes starting with Celestine II and ending with the 111th Pope, who remains unknown as yet.

St. Malachi was born in 1905 in the town of Armagh, Ulster, Ireland. His real name was Mael Maedoc ua Morgair. Apparently he was born to the priesthood because even in school he surpassed his teachers in knowledge and in saintliness. Still a boy, he joined the hermit Ismar Armagh, a small religious community. It had its center in the cell of the hermit. St. Malachi's devout studies brought him to the attention of the Bishop of Armagh, Celsius, who ordained the young man a priest and a deacon.

Malachi rose quickly in the service of God. In no time at all he was made Abbott of Bangor. The job was not an easy one. The monastery had grown neglected and Malachi had a lot to do to put it to right. But he did, and did it so well that God conferred on him the dual gift of miracle and prophecy.

Eventually, Malachi became the Archbishop of Armagh. In later years he visited Rome, where it was said that he wrote some exceedingly strange prophecies, many of them dealing with the Popes.

***

THE STORY BEHIND ST. MALACHI'S PROPHECIES

Oddly enough, the holy man's work remained unpublished for nearly 500 years. According to legend, a Dominican friar named Arnold de Wion published a book of prophecies that were said to be the work of the Irish monk. Wion said that Malachi completed the manuscript in Rome and that he showed it to Pope Innocent II, who approved of it and placed it in the Vatican archives. Wion published it in 1595, five hundred years after Malachi's birth. Wion merely dragged the script out of its dusty niche, brushed it off and published it.

***

MALACHI'S LATIN MOTTOES

The old manuscript consists of one hundred and eleven brief latin mottoes, each allegedly identifying each Pope in succession, starting with Celestine II, who lived during Malachi's time.

The last pope, still in the future, was described as "the time of the end." Malachi ends his long list of prophecies with the following words: "During the last persecution of the Holy Roman Church there shall sit the Roman Peter, who shall feed the sheep amid great tribulations, and when these are

passed, the City of the Seven Hills shall be utterly destroyed and the awful Judge will judge the people."

***

FACT OR FORGERY?

There are some scholars who believe the above passage is a forgery, and even that the entire manuscript is a forgery. Their contention is that the work was written by Dominican friars. Their theory is that the prophetic mottoes were strangely accurate between 1095 and 1595, when the work was published, but that accuracy fails after that latter date.

What these scholars fail to take into account is the fact that even after the work was published, Malachi's mottoes seemed to fit. Admittedly, in a few cases the references made by the Irish monk are rather vague, but there are enough of them which do appear to have pinpoint accuracy. Examine them for yourself.

***

POPE LEO XI

Malachi dealt early with Pope Leo XI. The Spanish Pope's real name was Alessandro de' Medici-Ottaviano. He was a patron of the arts and was a son of a niece of Leo X. Malachi's motto for Pope Leo XI was "Wave-man: Like the wind he came, and like the water he went."

The prophecy could not have been more accurate. Pope Leo XI reigned for only 27 days. He was Pope from April 1, 1605 to April 27, 1605. His election had been approved on all sides and there was great sorrow when he died.

It's also interesting to note the dates. Leo XI died 100 years after Malachi was born.

***

POPE PAUL V

Pope Paul V succeeded Leo XI and sat on the Throne of St. Peter from May 16, 1605 to January 28, 1621. Malachi's prophecy for him was two short words: "Perverse People."

The phrase may sound obscure until you realize that Paul V had problems with certain people at the very beginning of his pontificate. There was a sharp dispute with Venice. A state church was created and persecutions were taking place. A war was threatened, with English and German Protestants ready to fight on the side of Venice. Henry IV of France stepped in and offered a compromise which saw the Pope and the Church defeated.

The situation worsened when Henry IV was murdered in 1610. Pope Paul V was accused by England of hatching the Gunpowder Plot, a desperate plan of persecutions which was actually denounced by the Church. Persecutions spread all the way to Ireland. The Pope then saw the outbreak of the Thirty

POPE CLEMENT XIII

Years' War.

Malachi certainly appears to have come close when he suggested that Pope Paul V would have to deal with "Perverse People."

**

POPE ALEXANDER VII

This Pope's real name was Fabio Chigi and he headed the church from April 7, 1655 to May 22, 1667. He had a coffin and skull made and placed in his room to remind him of human frailty.

Malachi's motto for him was "Guardian of the Hills." How could the Irish monk know, 150 years later, that a Pope would reign whose family arms portrayed three hills watched over by a star?

**

POPE CLEMENT X

Clement pontificate lasted from April 29, 1670 to July 22, 1676, only six years. Malachi's motto for him was "Concerning the Mighty River."

Prophetic? It certainly was! When Clement was a baby he nearly drowned when the Tiber overflowed its banks and flooded his home. He was almost swept away by the rushing water. The quick action of his nurse, who grabbed him at the last instant, saved his life.

Malachi must have had a real vision with Clement because the Pope's family arms depicts the Milky Way. The Latin name for Milky Way is "magnum flumen," or "great river."

**

POPE INNOCENT XIII

Innocent came from an extremely religious family. He was educated by the Jesuits. His character was irreproachable. Innocent was one of the most religious of all Popes to that time.

Malachi's motto for him was "Of Good Religion."

**

POPE BENEDICT XIII

Benedict's family produced only soldiers. His pontificate lasted from May 29, 1724 to February 21, 1730, and although he was a saintly man himself, he was surrounded by evil men who enriched themselves through corruption.

Malachi's motto for Pope Benedict XIII was "Soldier in Battle."

**

POPE CLEMENT XII

Clement headed the church from July 12, 1730 to February 6, 1740. During his pontificate he purchased the busts of the emperors from the collection of the well-known Cardinal Alessandro Albani. He laid the foundations of the Capitoline Museum, which was the first archeological museum in Europe. He also built the Fontana Trevi and the facade of the Lateran Basilica. One of

the most beautiful chapels in the world—the Capella Corsini—was built by Clement XII.

Malachi's motto for him was "The Column is Raised Up."

***

POPE CLEMENT XIII

At times St. Malachi was uncanny in his prophecies, and describing Clement XIII was one of them. The Pope reigned from July 6, 1758 to February 2, 1769, and his real name was Carlo Rezzonico. He was the 94th Pope. Before his pontificate began he lived in Umbria. Unbria's symbol was a rose.

Malachi's motto for Clement was "Rose of Umbria."

***

POPE CLEMENT XIV

Malachi's accuracy was shown again with Clement XIV. This Pope headed the church from May 19, 1769 to September 22, 1774. A persistant rumor suggests that he died by poisoning, but it has no basis in fact. Clement's escutcheon or Family Arms shows a running bear.

Malachi wrote of him, "Ursus Velox," or "Swift Bear."

***

POPE PIUS VII

Pius VII headed the church for only a short time—March 31, 1829 to November 30, 1830. When he was a Bishop, Pius VII predicted that he would be Pius VIII. Only one encyclical was attributed to Pius VIII and it dealt with laxity in religion.

Malachi's words for him were: "Religious Man."

***

POPE GREGORY XVI

This Pope came from a religious order in Etruria. He specialized in archaeological research. He was particularly interested in the "balnea," or ancient baths, for which the province was famous.

Somehow, Malachi was aware of that fact even though Pope Gregory lived 300 years after Malachi's death. The Irish monk wrote of Pope Gregory XVI: "Concerning the Baths of Etruria."

***

POPE LEO XIII

This Pope's pontificate lasted from 1878 to 1903. His crest was a comet on an azure field. Malachi knew it would be because his motto for Pope Leo XIII was a "A Light in the Sky."

***

POPE BENEDICT XV

It was with this Pope that St. Malachi really hit the nail on the head.

Benedict was the 104th Pope. His pontificate began on September 3, 1914 and ended on January 22, 1922.

The year 1914 saw the outbreak of World War I. For the next four years millions of Christians would die on the battlefields. Then in 1917 the start of the Russian Revolution was another strong set-back for Christians. At that time more than 200 million people turned away from Christianity to embrace the new "religion" in Soviet Russia.

Malachi's motto for Benedict XV was: "Religion Depopulated."

***

POPE PIUS XI

Pius XI's most pressing problem was the struggle against Communist purges in Russia, Spain and Mexico. These purges zeroed in on the Catholic Church. The bloody persecutions of the Catholics in Germany started in 1933 and lasted until the end of World War II. Pius XI. was so furious with Adolph Hitler that when the German dictator visited Rome in 1938 the Pope refused to see the murderer of thousands of innocent people. Pius XI closed the Vatican and left Rome. He died in 1939, still trying to stop the madman in Germany from denying freedom to thousands of people.

Malachi's motto for him was "Intrepid Faith."

***

POPE PIUS XII

We said earlier that Pope Pius XII was a visionary Pope, a faith healer and a clairvoyant. We also said that many people, even non-Catholics, regard him as a saint.

Malachi's motto fit him perfectly: "Angelic Pastor."

***

POPE JOHN XXIII

"Papa John" as he was lovingly called is a mystery to proponents of Malachi's prophecies. The monk's motto for John XXIII was "Pastor and Sailor," however, there is nothing in the Pope's background or pontificacy to indicate that he was a sailor.

***

POPE PAUL VI

Paul VI is the 108th Pope. Malachi described him as the "Flower of Flowers." The prophecy is rather vague. So far, Malachi appears to have missed his mark. Nevertheless, that does not mean that he was wrong. Something yet may turn up about Paul VI that will have some significance.

***

POPE JOHN PAUL II

The world knows much about John Paul II. Apparently so did St. Malachi. Shortly after 5:00 p.m. on May 13, 1981, Pope John Paul II was shot while

riding in a white jeep through St. Peter's Square.

The man who shot him was Mehmet Ali Agca, a Turk.

Malachi's brief words for Pope John Paul II were: "Concerning the Crescent Moon." Many have taken that to mean a threat from the Arab or Moslem World.

But it was a Turk who caused the Pope injury. And if you look at the Turkish flag you will see a crescent moon and a star on a red field!

***

ONLY TWO POPES REMAIN

Malachi's 110th Pope was given the motto: "Of the Labor of the Sun." The motto for the 111th Pope is: "Of the Glory of the Olive." It was the monk's last motto.

Does it mean that the end of Christianity will come when the last Pope closes his pontificate reign? Stewart Robb, a Nostradamus scholar and an expert on the Malachi prophecies, refers to the last prophecy, "Of the Glory of the Olive" when he says: "It could mean the inception of lasting peace, this being the connotation of the olive branch, or since the olive is a symbol of the Holy Land, any glorification of the Holy Land might indicate a resurgence of true Christianity."

***

THE LAST POPE, 1999, AND NOSTRADAMUS

Stewart Robb's view is optimistic, and hopes he is right. But the subject of his intense studies—Nostradamus—has a more frightening prophecy in store for us in 1999.

First of all, the year 1999 would likely bring us to the last Pope. We can assume by mathematical formula (the average reign of our Popes), that the last one will be in office at about the year 1999.

And we can apply a Nostradamus quatrain which is quite alarming:
In the year 1999 in the seventh month,
A great king of frightfulness will come from the skies
To resuscitate the great king of Angoumois,
Around this time Mars will reign for the good cause.

Qualified interpreters read this to mean that a horrendous war will take place at that time. Angoumois refers to France, and that she will not engage in such a war without her traditional allies beside her. Having a king come from the skies won't be unusual in 1999 because interplanetary travel will be commonplace. The appearance of the king, however, will greatly help the cause of the allies.

***

REVIEW OF MALACHI'S DE GLORIA OLIVAE

One point we have to take into account is Malachi's detailed description of

the last Pope. He said more about this one than about any other. The phrase, "Of the Glory of the Olive" was expanded on by the Irish monk. He added: "During the final persecution of the Holy Roman Church, there will sit upon the throne Peter the Roman, who will pasture his flock in the midst of many tribulations; with these passed, the city of the seven hills will be destroyed; and the awful Judge will then judge the people."

That passage certainly ties in with the quatrain of Nostradamus. It is not at all optimistic, and it does not supply us with any hope that the olive in this case refers to lasting peace.

***

ANOTHER EXPLANATION

In his book, "The Story of Prophecy," Henry James Foreman writes:

"The prophecy of St. Malachi regarding the last of all the Popes is more explicit than most; Peter, the Roman, will lead his sheep to pasture in the midst of numerous tribulations; the City of the Seven Hills will be destroyed. The twilight settles—indeed, the depth of night—before the promised dawn!

"The End of the Ages will be upon the world and the last persecution, the most terrible of all, will afflict the church. The tribulations will be as great as those which overtook the Jews at the end of the destruction of Jerusalem by Titus. So devastating indeed will they be, that, in the words of St. Matthew: 'And except be no flesh saved; but for the elect's sake those days shall be shortened.'

"But not Peter the Roman, nor any number of just men, shall avail to save the Eternal City!

"Many commentators do not like to believe, in spite of the prophecies, that this Peter is actually to mark the end of the papacy. They believe that only a sort of hiatus will ensue, and then a glorious recrudescence. Mostly, however, this prophecy is taken literally, in common with all others bearing upon the predecessors of Peter the Roman. And that being so, does it mean that the End of the Ages, as prophesied in the Gospels, and in many other places, is actually at hand?

"With only seven more Popes (now two more Popes since Foreman's book was written), after the present one, that dreadful period looms ominously near. St. Malachi's prophecy begins with Pope Celestin II in the 12th Century. Since then in a period of 779 years there have been 94 Popes (up to the time this book was written), up to Pius XI, giving an average of eight years for the reign of each Pope. Even if we increase the average to say nine years, owing to greater statistical expectation of life in more recent times, only sixty-three years of the papacy would remain after the present Pope (Pius XI). We know, of course, that some Popes have had long reigns. Pope Leo XIII, for example, sat in the Vatican for a quarter of a century, and Pius

IX ruled for thirty-two years. We are now, however, considering averages. Sixty-three years is the equivalent of but two generations. One generation of this century has already more than passed. Two more generations bring the time to the end of the century, or roughly to about the year 2000.

"The great Pyramid (in Egypt) dating does not run beyond the year 2001. Nostradamus fixes the year 1999 as the time for an attack and one of the terrible destructions of the city of Paris, by a strange people coming from the north, perhaps Asia. St. Malachi and the monk Padua predict the burning of Rome at the end of the papacy, which seems to fall at about the same period. Many other prophecies point to the 'End of the Age' as falling within the present century. One cannot but recall the words of the Gospel according to St. Mark: 'Verily I say unto you that this generation shall not pass till all these things be done.' "

* * *

JEANE DIXON'S PROPHECY FOR 1999

Jeane Dixon, businesswoman and author, is the best known of modern psychics. Being very religious, she relies on visions from God, but also receives premonitions in dreams. She occasionally uses a crystal ball. She says she has seen the future to 2037.

According to Jeane Dixon, 1988 will see the end of a long Israel-Arab war. At that time, Russia and her satellite armies will move in and occupy the lands of all of the participants in that war. There will be bloodshed for seven more years. The United States won't interfere because it will be too weak economically and militarily.

In 1995, the United States, England, France, Germany and Japan, will set up headquarters in Rome to begin a counter offensive against Russia and the Middle East.

In 1999 we see the kind of destruction talked about by Nostradamus. Jeane Dixon says that in this year the United States will be at war with Russia and its satellites. A nuclear holocaust in the form of bombs will rain down on American coastal cities, both east and west. Russian missiles, launched from the Carpathians, will devastate the cities of Europe (here we have confirmation of Paris and Rome being destroyed).

According to Dixon's prophecy, we will see a phenomenon similar to the stand of Moses at the Red Sea in Israel's early history. God will intervene and Russian leaders will find that this divine intervention is far superior to their armies.

In the year 2000 the Russian forces in Israel will be surrounded and destroyed by the United States and its allies, still based in Rome. Israel will

be saved. Peace will reign.

The leader in Rome will be hailed as a savior, ruler and a great conquering hero. But who is he? Dixon doesn't say that he is a Pope, but she does describe him.

***

JEANE DIXON'S PROPHECY

She says, "A child was born somewhere in the Middle East shortly after 7:00 a.m. (EST) on February 5, 1962 and will revolutionize the world. Before the close of the century he will bring together all mankind in one all-embracing faith. This will be the foundation of a new Christianity, with every sect and creed united through this man who will walk among the people to spread the wisdom of the Almighty Power.

"This person," continues Dixon, "though born of humble peasant origin, is a descendant of Queen Nefertiti and her Pharaoh husband; of this I am sure. There was nothing kingly about his coming—no kings or shepherds to do homage to this new-born baby—but he is the answer to the prayers of a troubled world. Mankind will begin to feel the great force of this man in the early 1980s and during the subsequent ten years of the world as we know it will be reshaped and revamped into one without wars or suffering. His power will grow great until 1999, at which time the peoples of the earth will probably discover the full meaning of the vision."

***

WHAT FULL MEANING?

Jeane Dixon tells us that by 1999 this man in Rome will prove to be a "false prophet of evil." Whatever evil he does will be corrected when Jesus Christ will be seen bodily in the Holy Land, at which time all Jews will proclaim him the true Messiah.

This intriguing man coming from the Middle East undoubtedly won't be Peter the Roman, the last Pope, but it is easy to speculate that he might bring about the end of Christianity, and the line of Popes.

Many of Jeane Dixon's prophecies have come true; we can only wait and see if her predictions for 1999 are accurate.

* * *

THE STRANGE STORY OF POPE JOAN

You are not likely to find any reference to the woman who was a Pope in religious history books. She has been excluded. Does it mean that she didn't exist? Hardly. All it means is that the medieval chroniclers who wrote about her have been discredited.

But there were many writers in those ancient days who did write about Pope Joan, and they did not do so in vague terms. Many of the accounts were quite detailed, and all of them contained the same biographical data.

What we can do here is relate what was said about her and then let you be the judge as to whether she really existed.

***
MARIANUS SCOTUS

This writer was the first to mention Pope Joan in his chronicles. He inserted the following passage:

"A.D. 854, Lotharii 14, Joanna, a woman, succeeded Leo, and reigned two years, five months, and four days."

Admittedly, Scotus was sparing in his remarks about the woman. It's important to remember that he was not her contemporary and that he died A. D. 1086, some three hundred years after her reign.

It's also important to remember that if he had lied, why had he bothered to do so in one sentence? As a writer wishing to foster a lie on his public, why hadn't he embellished the falsehood? When one looks at that simple sentence, one gets the notion that he was stating a fact that he had found in a musty volume and did not expand on it because there was nothing there on which to expand. What he apparently hoped for was that a future researcher would take his lead and dig further into the woman's history. Someone did.

***
SIGEBERT de GEMBLOURS

This writer, who died on October 5, 1112, found reference to Pope Joan in the work of Anastasius the librarian. Gemblours dug into the story and wrote: "It is reported that this John (Joan) was a female, and that she conceived by one of her servants. The Pope, becoming pregnant, gave birth to a child; wherefore some do not number her among the Pontiffs."

***
THE STORY SPREADS

Other writers of the day picked up where Gemblours left off and researched it. Otto of Frisingen and Gotfrid of Viterbo write about the lady Pope in their histories. Then Martin Polonus offered more details.

He wrote: "After Leo IV, John Anglus, a native of Metz, reigned two years, five months, and four days. And the pontificate was vacant for a month. He died in Rome. He is related to have been a female, and, when a girl, to have accompanied her sweetheart in male costume to Athens; there she advanced in various sciences, and none could be found equal her. So, after having studied for three years in Rome, she had great masters for her pupils and hearers. And when there arose a high opinion in the city of her virtue and knowledge, she was unanimously elected Pope. But during her Papacy she became in the family way by a familiar. Not knowing the time of birth, as she was on her way from St. Peter's to the Lateran she had a painful delivery, between the Coliseum and St. Clement's Church, in the street. Having died after, it is said that she was buried on the spot; and therefore the Lord Pope always turns aside from that way, it is supposed by some out of detestation for what happened there. Nor on that account is she placed in the catalogue of the Holy Pontiffs, not only on account of her sex, but also because of the horribleness of the circumstance."

***

WHAT WAS JOAN'S REAL NAME

One writer, John Huss, is convinced that Joan's real name was Agnes or Hagnes, and that one of these two was her baptismal name. Other researchers feel the woman's name was Gilberta.

In any event, wood engravings were carved depicting the graphic account of her giving birth in the street. One such engraving can be found in a book titled "Puerperium Johannis Papae 8, 1530."

***

DID JOAN NEGOTIATE WITH AN ANGEL?

It is said that moments before Joan gave birth to her baby she was visited by an angel who offered her a grim choice. According to Stephen Blauch, who stated in his "Urbis Romae Mirabilia," the angel asked her to choose whether she would burn eternally in hell or have her confinement in public. Wisely, Joan chose the latter.

***

WHO FATHERED JOAN'S BABY?

Originally, the man was a servant. But there were many anti-christs about in those days and they saw to it that the baby was sired by a Cardinal. Some said the Devil himself impregnated Joan. What was generally agreed upon at the time of the actual birth was that a Satan-like creature was seen fluttering and crowing overhead.

***

THE WORDS OF MOSHEIM

This writer said in his "Ecclesiastical History," "Between Leo IV, who

died 855, and Benedict III, a woman who concealed her sex and assumed the name of John, it is said, opened her way to the Pontifical throne by her learning and genius, and governed the Church for a time. She is commonly called the Papess Joan. During the five subsequent centuries the witnesses to this extraordinary event are without number; nor did anyone prior to the Reformation by Luther, regard the thing as either incredible or disgraceful to the Church."

**

DOUBTERS' ARGUMENTS

There are many devil's advocates in the story of Pope Joan. One strong argument concerns Marianus Scotus, the writer who first brought Pope Joan to light. Scotus died in 1086. He was a monk of St. Martin of Cologne, and later of Fulda, and finally of St. Alban's, at Metz. Doubters ask how Scotus could have found documents so far from Rome. And they wanted to know what document existed on which he based his research.

As for Sigebert de Gemblours, this man lived two and a half centuries after Pope Joan. He died in 1112. Many students feel his manuscripts were tampered with.

***

HISTORY OFFERS NO PLACE FOR JOAN

We did say earlier that history does not record Joan's reign. If you look at a list of popes you will find Leo IV died on July 17, 855. Benedict III was consecrated on September 1 of the same year. There does not appear to be any way you can squeeze Pope Joan between Leo and Benedict. Yet she was supposed to have reigned for two years, five months and four days.

***

FLY IN THE OINTMENT

At this point we learn that there actually was a Pope who reigned between Leo and Benedict. He was an antipope and his name was Anastasius the Librarian, mentioned earlier. Anastasius was one of the first to write about Pope Joan.

***

WHO WAS ANASTASIUS?

This man was elected immediately upon the death of Leo. Anastasius seized the Lateran by force and occupied the palace of the Popes. He owed his election to Emperor Louis, who insisted on Anastasius' papacy. Apparently, Anastasius guessed that Benedict was next in line for the Throne of St. Peter because he maltreated him and then imprisoned Benedict.

Fortunately, the reign of this antipope was short-lived. Two days, in fact. All parties rejected him and then threw him out of the palace. Benedict was then elected Pope. Being a mild-mannered man, he pardoned Anastasius and

made him an abbot.

***

WAS ANASTASIUS POPE JOAN?

That theory was bandied about for awhile, but it has no basis in fact. No documents in the archives even hint that the antipope was a woman. No charges were ever made against the antipope concerning his sex.

***

JOAN'S FULL STORY

She was born in Engelheim, Saxony and was christened either Agnes, Hagnes, Gerberta, Gilberta, Joanna, Margaret, Isabel, Dorothy or Jutt. She was the daughter of an English missionary who left England to preach the Gospel to the Saxons, who were recently converted.

Joan had a love of letters, so much so that at an early age she was considered a genius. She fell madly in love with a young monk in Fulda. This passion was so great that she left her parents and ran off with the monk. To do so without raising eyebrows, she dressed herself as a man.

In Fulda, Joan divided her time between her lover and the musty books in the monastery. The arrangement worked well for a time, but she found herself growing restless with conventional life. She wanted to see more of the world. She was also dissatisfied with the local library because there were no books on abstruse science. She convinced her monk that what they had to do was to leave Fulda and explore other countries, which they did.

They visited England, France and Italy. The couple then went to Athens, where Joan was in her glory. In this Greek city she was able to pursue her studies with an unflagging addiction. Her monk, however, did not travel well. He became sick and soon died in Joan's arms.

The young woman was devastated. It took her a long time to recover from the blow, but when she did she went to Rome. She had no skills, but she did have a vast storehouse of knowledge. She put it to good use by opening a school. In no time at all, Joan acquired a reputation of being a woman of learning and piety. Her devotion to her religion was widely known, so much so in fact that when Pope Leo IV died, she was unanimously elected Pope.

No one suspected her real sex. She used the name John VIII and apparently filled the chair adequately.

According to legend, Joan fell in love with a cardinal and became pregnant. And during the time of Rogation processions, Joan was seized with violent pains. She fell to the ground on the street between the amphitheater and St. Clement's. While attendants ministered to her, she delivered a son.

Here, the legend goes astray. Some writers say that mother and son died on

the spot. Others say that she survived and was jailed. Still others insist that the child was spirited away and that he will be the anti-christ of the last days.

In any event, a marble monument was erected on the spot where Joan gave birth. It depicted Joan and her baby. The monument was declared to be accursed to all ages.

Did Joan really exist? There is no hard and fast answer. We don't know if or how much the ancient writers embellished their stories, or if they were not above telling downright lies.

All we can say for sure is that she doesn't exist in the formal histories of the Church, but she certainly plays a large part in its mythology.

***

THE VATICAN

POPE BENEDICT XIV WROTE THE BOOK ON MIRACLES

What's the difference between the paranormal and the miraculous? That question has long been a bone of contention among theologians. But as far as the Church is concerned, the question was answered in the early 1700s by Prospero Cardinal Lambertini, who later became Pope Benedict XIV, when he wrote a dissertation on miracles. It is still considered the official church authority on the subject.

Actually, Lambertini wrote the book as a guide for papal authorities. These authorities were always being asked to investigate the miraculous deeds of people being considered for sainthood. As you know, for one to become a saint it is necessary that two proven miracles be attributed to him or her before beatification and two before canonization.

The Cardinal knew that there were many so-called miracles that were linked only to the human mind and that no divine power was invloved at all. Lambertini saw his task as separating the paranormal from the miraculous so that one could determine if an event was actually produced by God.

He therefore rejected phenomena like clairvoyance, telepathy and most healing. He did not consider them of divine origin. He did feel, however, that some forms of prophecy could come through the will of God. The Cardinal's definition of a miracle was an "event brought about by the supernatural order within the physical world."

Lambertini wrote that miracles included stigmata, bilocation (the human body being in two places at once), involuntary levitation, and some healings that were not produced by the traditional psychic healing practices.

He also included as miracles the miracles of nature, such as incorruptibility (the failure of the body to putrefy after death, the odor of sanctity (wondrous perfumes that emanate from the presence of saintly people), and images of Christ or others that have appeared on such physical objects as walls and pieces of cloth. And he also included the cases of Marian apparitions (appearances of the Holy Mother) if seen by more than one person at a time.

* * *

POPE PIUS IX

MIRACLES—RECENT AND ANCIENT

A picture of the Blessed Virgin Mary now enshrined at St. Paul's Greek Orthodox Church was found in an attic in Island Park, New York. The date was March 16, 1960. Mrs. Pagona Catsounis came across the framed lithograph by accident. She looked at the picture and saw that it was crying.

Mrs. Catsounis and her husband immediately called the Rev. George Papadea of St. Paul's in Hempstead. The priest hurried to the house.

He said later, "When I arrived a tear was drying beneath the left eye. Then I saw another tear well up in her left eye. It started as a small round globule of moisture in the corner of her left eye, and it slowly trickled down her face."

Within a week's time, more than 4,000 visitors came to the Catsounis house. The picture weeped for a full week. Father Papadeas blessed the house, and eventually took the picture to St. Paul's.

***

SHADOW ON THE WALL

A miracle occurred on May 18, 1975 in Holman, a small town in New Mexico. Two teenage boys were walking aimlessly around the Immaculate Heart of Mary Church when they noticed a rather odd-shaped shadow on one wall. They went closer to it, but did not stay to examine it in detail. They became frightened and ran away. What they saw was a figure of Christ's head and shoulders. It wasn't really a shadow, but a configuration existing in the texture of the concrete.

***

BRONZE FIGURE CRIED

Ever since Christianity spread throughout the world, there have been numerous cases of religious effigies found suddenly to weep or bleed. Religious statues, paintings, icons and lithographs that have cried or bled are thoroughly documented. However, not all cases are Christian. Allen Demetrius of Pittsburgh, Pennsylvania owns a Japanese bronze statue that was said to have wept on August 6, 1945, the day the atomic bomb was dropped on Hiroshima. And on March 18, 1979—10 days before the nuclear reactor accident at Three Mile Island—the statue wept again.

***

DIVINE IMAGE

When the divine image of the Virgin Mary appeared on a peasant's cloak in Mexico on December 12, 1531, the miracle became the most famous of all.

The cloak is still on display at the Basilica of Our Lady of Guadalupe in Villa Madero, a community only a few miles north of Mexico City.

The divine image on the cloak is as clear today as it was more than 400

years ago!

The peasant in question was an Indian who adopted the Spanish name of Juan Diego after he converted to Catholicism. The story actually began in the morning of December 8, 1531. Juan Diego passed a hill called Tepeyacac. At that moment he was stunned by a radiant apparition. The figure had a dark complexion and spoke to Diego in his own native tongue, which was Nahuatl.

The young man was awe-struck. He listened carefully when the apparition told him that she was the Virgin Mary and that she must tell the local bishop that she wanted a church built on the spot in her honor.

Juan Diego hurried to the bishop with his story, but was met with indifference. The bishop said he would believe him if the figure would prove her divine nature and mission with a "sign."

Juan Diego met the apparition a second time and told her what the bishop said. He needed something that would convince the man that she was actually the Virgin Mary.

Diego was told to climb the small hill on which she appeared. He did, and then saw something that was wondrous to behold. Instead of the usual weed-covered field which was also full of cacti, Diego saw a miraculous garden replete with flowers of all varieties and colors. All were in full bloom, even the Castilian roses from Spain, and all were out of season!

The lovely woman gathered a bouquet and placed it in Diego's cloak. She told the youth to take them to the bishop as a sign of her miraculous presence. She also warned Diego not to open the cloak in the presence of anyone but the bishop himself.

Again, Diego went to the bishop, this time carefully holding his cloak in his arms. He told the bishop about the apparition and what she had done with his cloak. He then opened his mantle so that the bouquet of flowers would fall to the ground. But there were no flowers. Instead, there was a treasure far greater.

The cloak held a full-color image of the Blessed Mother. The picture appeared to be stamped right into the cloth!

A church was built on the spot at which the Virgin Mary appeared. The cloak is still on display, with the image as life-like as it was more than 400 years ago. It has not faded, nor has the cloak's material—made of rough cloth from cactus fibre—disintegrated, which it should have done centuries ago!

Not long ago the miracle was investigated by the Image of Guadalupe Research Project, based in Florida. In February, 1979, Dr. Philip Callahan, a biophysicist at the University of Florida, inspected the image with the aid of special film akin to infrared. His tests revealed that the image has no underdrawn blueprint and that there are no brush strokes on the image itself. These tests show that the image was not painted on, as scoffers over

the years claimed.

***

IMAGE IN CHRISTCHURCH

Dean Liddell was a well-known British preacher at Christchurch Cathedral in Oxford. He died in 1898. Before his death he had installed a decorative window in the church in honor of his deceased daughter. Faithful parishioners installed plaques in the same area to honor the Liddell family. In 1921 a white stain formed near the tablets. At the end of two years the stain had formed itself into a definite likeness of the preacher.

***

SPECTACULAR FACES

The best documented cases in recent history concerns itself with a rash of spectacular faces which formed on the floor of a small house in the town of Belmez de la Moraleda, Spain. The year was 1971. The faces were religious in nature and were subjected to an intense investigation by Hans Bender, one of Germany's leading parapsychologists. The phenomenon lasted until 1974, and by that time dozens of faces emerged on the floor.

Curious villagers finally dug up the hearth and found human bones. A check into the town's history revealed that the house had been built on an old cemetery site that held the remains of Christian martyrs killed by the Moors in the 11th Century.

***

THE POPE

Who is he? He is the one person in the world who stands for the hope of an international organization to bring about the rightful unity of the people of the world. He affirms the principle of international law. His is the most important voice which warns of the threat of atomic war. He is the voice of universal conscience, and the advocate of hunted humanity in the demonic period of fear and among the most fearful collapses in history. He is the indestructible and sure rock of peace.

POPE LEO XI

Benefit of Clergy

OF all the vexing questions surrounding the widespread and on-going clergy sexual abuse crisis in the Roman Catholic Church, perhaps the ones involving the Pope are among those most begging for an answer. For such a centralized, authoritarian organization headed by one single man, the Pope, the key Watergate-type question of "what did he know and when did he know it?" is crucial to any understanding of the full dimensions of the crisis.

The Roman Catholic Church has a long tradition of policing its own, however poorly it may have done the job. The hierarchy fought hard for the privilege as soon as Christianity was first legalized by the Roman Empire, and has guarded it jealously ever since. During the Middle Ages, in most countries, clerics were to be tried in ecclesiastical courts, and if found guilty, sent to ecclesiastical prisons run by the Inquisition.

This is the origin of the phrase "benefit of clergy" – not for the good of other prisoners, but for any priest or monk apprehended by the sheriff. If a man could prove he was educated by reading Latin from the parish Bible, he was presumed to be a cleric and turned over to the diocesan authorities. Only in cases of flagrant heresy, which was considered treason to the state as well, would a cleric be turned back over or "relaxed" to the secular officials in order to be burnt, so that the actual death sentence would not taint the Church.

The Church thus developed its own elaborate legal system which served as the basis for the Inquisition in its many forms.

It also developed its own penitentiary system – monasteries and convents of "strict observance" – which were not just for extremely devout ascetics who enjoyed wearing hair shirts and sleeping on boards, but where convicted priests, monks, nuns and even laypeople could be effectively watched and punished out of the sight of the faithful and the government, all for the good of their souls.

Vatican Secret Archives

In any case, records of clerical hijinks were kept in the secret archives of the diocese, which even now is mandated by Canon Law. The Vatican also has its own Secret Archives (their unashamed, actual name), which are as vast as they are old. Headed by a cardinal like the Vatican Library, another rumored storehouse of secrets, they partially open today to a few approved scholars who are let in only with specific purposes and with permission of the Pope.

It is the most mysterious institution in the papal city, for in its more than thirty miles of shelving are reputed to be the accumulated records of scandals, secrets, and revelations of the most shocking and explosive kind, blithely boxed and filed away with the insouciance born of centuries of silence and discretion.

The Secret Archives are so vast, disorganized, and secret that no one even knows their full extent — one expert claims that there are "only" 24 miles or so of shelves, though the Vatican itself recently admitted that there are "85 linear kilometers (52 miles) of shelves".

She says that there are 135 fondi, or individual archives. These include not only records of papal decrees, chancery business, and the like, but much other material, including the records of prominent papal families, suppressed religious orders and monasteries, and those of nunciatures, or church embassies. Most of this has never been examined, much less indexed and cataloged.

There have been several attempts to create indices by past archivists, but they were incomplete to begin with. The archives have been moved and looted several times during their long history. Most of the medieval records that survived the Babylonian Captivity were lost during the Sack of Rome in the sixteenth century; Napoleon took them to Paris in the eighteenth where many volumes were recycled into butcher paper; and much fell into the hands of the Italian government later on.

Moreover, the paperwork generated by the various curial organizations, while technically belonging to the Secret Archives, remains under the control and often in the possession of the dicastery that produced it. Thus the records of the Inquisition, for example, can only be seen with permission from its successor organization, the Sacred Congregation for the Propagation of the Faith, as well as that of the archivists.

Access to the archives is strictly controlled, and the period when records cannot be examined is long, even by institutional standards: everything since Napoleon was judged to be "too recent", at least in the 1960s.

Could There be Truly Secret, Secret Archives?

The Italian anticlerical party was disappointed in its hope of finding the Secret Archives a repository for records of usurpations, crimes, and sexual perversions. But the question still remains as to whether the Secret Archives exercises internal censorship over its materials.

What action is taken by a scriptor, custodian, or prefect when, in the course of his work, he comes across material that is morally or theologically controversial? Has a closed (chiuso) fondo [individual archive] gradually accumulated, the much-talked-of fondo about which nothing is actually known, a closed fondo which is categorically denied by the Archives authorities?

This is a question which puzzled me during the long time I spent working in the Secret Archives, and to which I still have not found any answer. My own personal impression is that no such material is destroyed.

The men of the Archives have too much sense of the past, too much reverence for scholarship, too much obligation to learning, for that. But such documents may be omitted from the inventories, bound in volumes containing documents of a very different kind, and relegated to some fondo that is closed because of chronological limitation or very seldom consulted.

This happened with the personal letters of Pope Borgia to the little clan of his devoted women, and with the original summary of the process of [the trial of] Giordano Bruno, and may have happened many other times that we do not know about. Such documents may eventually reappear in the future...[3]

Once in the Vatican, certainly the Secret Archives are central as the final repository of all the reports of all kinds of dirty deeds done by clergy, but as archives, they would not be responsible for dealing with current cases. Still, the Curia is quite protective of its contents — several years ago an approved priest, Fr. Filipo Tamburini, who had worked there for a dozen years, was banned for writing Saints and Sinners, a book about cases from the Secret Archives of erring clergy who lived four or five centuries ago.

Truly, Rome holds its secrets most jealously.

Cardinals swear an oath when they first get the red hat to preserve the secrets of the Church. So trying to find out which officials in the Vatican, if any, are dealing with these questions is much like trying to understand the inner workings of the Kremlin in the old days, or, for that matter, who in the U.S. government really knows what about UFOs.

To outsiders, such institutions present a blank outer wall and an impenetrable inner maze of arcane titles and unwritten rules, truly Byzantine in its complexity. Glimpses and outright guessing are sometimes the only means of constructing even a hypothetical picture of who or what is involved.

When in Rome

From the organizational chart of the Holy See,[4] the most likely place would seem to be the Sacred Congregation for the Doctrine of the Faith, which not that long ago was called the Holy Office of the Inquisition. That dicastery, however, seems to be concerned more with keeping theologians under control than sexual perpetrators.

Other likely Congregations would seem to be ones for the Clergy or the Institutes of Consecrated Life and Societies for the Apostolic Life (professed religious) or even Divine Worship and the Discipline of the Sacraments. (The Vatican has never gone for short, convenient titles.)

These are concerned with "the life, discipline, rights, and duties of the clergy" and members of religious orders while the latter deals with "abuses to the sacred liturgy."

Possibly they might have some jurisdiction, but perhaps the most likely institution to have anything to do with handling these crisis would be one of the Vatican's three ecclesiastical tribunals:

- **The Apostolic Penitentiary**

- **The Apostolic Signatura**

- **The Roman Rota**

The Rota deals with big-name divorces, while the Signatura is the "Supreme Court" of the Vatican. That leaves the Apostolic Penitentiary, which, despite its name, is not a prison for erring evangelists, but the oldest tribunal of the Holy See, in charge of granting absolutions, dispensations and other favors. (It also determines indulgences.)

The cardinal-prefect in charge, known as the Major (or formerly, Grand) Penitentiary of the Holy Roman Church, "is the only Curia official who remains in power, with the full authority of his office, during the Sede Vacante" [the period between popes].

This is so that he may continue to confer necessary pardon and dispensations during the duration of the vacancy.

"[He] is also the only cardinal that who may maintain a steady stream of outside contact as the nature of his office requires his continued attention. 'In the event he dies during Conclave, the conclavists must immediately elect a successor for the duration of the Conclave. The mystery of the mercy of God, which is exercised through the Penitentiary, thus does not suffer interruption.'"

It is generally thought that nobody, but nobody, could communicate with the cardinals in Conclave — that being the whole point of it. Indeed, the new rules are full of precautions that those in conclave have no means of communication with the outside world (such as cell phones), or that the Conclave is bugged.

Yet this Cardinal Penitentiary, currently William Wakefield Cardinal Baum, is considered so important to the life of the Church that he alone of all his peers will keep doing his job when the Pope dies, even during Conclave. He even has his own revolving drum dumbwaiter, smaller than the one used to pass food and medicine into the sequestered cardinals, to pass his secret documents through.

However, May Ying Welsh, a researcher in Rome, contends that many other cardinals retain their offices.

"These are the Cardinal Camerlengo, the Cardinal Vicar of the diocese of Rome, the Cardinal ArchPriest of St. Peter's Basilica, the Sostituto (Chief of Staff) of the Secretariat of State, and the Secretaries of each of the dicasteries of the curia. The Supreme Tribunal of the Apostolic Signatura (the Church's Supreme Court) and the Tribunal of the Roman Rota also continue their operations. Instead of reporting to the Pope, they all report to the College of Cardinals."

Others, she says, also have contact with the outside, though in all cases it is only in cases of emergency. She dismissed the idea that the rules cited above makes the Apostolic Penitentiary even more significant than the Pope, even though filling his position takes precedence even over the election of a new pontiff.

Ms. Welsh maintains that it is necessary for the Major Penitentiary to be in touch with the outside world in order to be able to forgive those on their deathbeds. There is some sense to this, I must admit. Still the question remains, is the Major Penitentiary, then, the cardinal in charge of maintaining the cover-up?

She also says this about the work of the Cardinal Penitentiary:

"The Major Penitentiary does not have a busy office. His work is extremely limited and mostly involves excommunications reserved to the Holy See. These are considered especially grave crimes.

The excommunications reserved to the Holy See fall into 5 categories:

1. For a Bishop who consecrates a Bishop without permission from the Holy See.

2. For desecration of the Eucharist.

3. For a priest breaking the confidentiality of a confession.

4. For a priest absolving his accomplice in a sexual sin.

4. For a person physically attacking the Pope."

Indeed, these are the provisions of Canon Law. It should be noted that in many cases that have come to light in the current clergy sex scandals, sexually predatory priests have heard the confessions of their victims, to fix the blame on the victim and ensure it stays secret. And of course, desecration of the Eucharist is one of the major points of the Black Mass.

Both these offenses are reserved to Rome. Yet, as far as I have been able to tell, in not a single one of these cases has the Vatican acted publicly to excommunicate the offender.

Thus, though the noble goal of silence may be to spare the faithful from scandal, it is a cover-up nonetheless, and the Major Penitentiary remains one of the prime suspects.

Papal Paperwork and Black Magic

A most telling clue that seems to confirm this comes from a journalistic peek through the crack between the basilica's doors. The following is excerpted from a book called Pontiff, a colorful insider's view of the Vatican from the last days of Paul VI through the assassination attempt on John Paul II. This scene deals with the Pope's daily paperwork in July, 1978.

Much of the work near the bottom of the tray requires no more than careful reading and initialing.

According to ***The Church Visible: The Ceremonial Life and Protocol of the Roman Catholic Church*** by James-Charles Noonan, Jr., the Apostolic Penitentiary handles complex problems of conscience:

"...It also advises the penalties a pope may impose for such a dire crime as a priest saying a black mass. Every year there are a number of such cases; they frighten Paul more than anything else. He regards them as proof the devil is alive and well and hiding inside the Church. Cardinal Giuseppe Paupini [the Major Penitentiary]... is the Vatican's resident expert on sorcery of all kinds. His work is adjudged so important and urgent that he will be the only cardinal allowed during the next Conclave to remain in contact with his office."

This has some very interesting and horrible implications. At the very least it should be rather disconcerting that the Pope, as part of his day-to-day job, is far more aware of the extent of true evil "hiding inside" the Church than even the most cynical outsiders can even imagine, and takes it very seriously.

Since John Paul II has retained such arrangements for the conclave after him, then it seems that it was no co-incidence that Paul's point man on clerical black magic was the chief pardoner of the Church. It makes sense that the Major Penitentiary would merit such consideration only if the papacy takes the threat of wicked clergy most seriously indeed and believes constant vigilance and total secrecy are necessary. One may further infer from the language used in the anecdote that this is not a new situation at all, and that such "dire crimes" seem to have grown throughout Paul's pontificate, at least.

Perhaps it is easy to read too much into all this. But if the current clergy sexual abuse crisis has revealed anything about the Roman Catholic Church, it's that the hierarchy can and will go to great lengths to hide its dirty laundry.

It has millennia of experience, and it just may be covering up even more monstrous secrets than anything revealed so far.

On April 30, 2001 (a noted satanic holiday), Pope John Paul II issued a new document as a result of the numerous new cases of priests accused of serious crimes in the wake of the scandals. The document, *Sacramentorum Sanctitatis Tutela*, gives the handling of cases formerly reserved for the pope's own decision over to the jurisdiction of the Congregation for the Doctrine of the Faith.

These include..."The sexual abuse of minors, crimes concerning the Eucharist, such as the sacrilegious use of the host, and crimes concerning the confessional, such as soliciting sex from someone who has come to a priest for confession."

As that dicastery used to be known as the Holy Office of the Inquisition, a Vatican spokesman acknowledged that it was because they had the "experience" necessary.

The trials, of course, would continue to be held in secret.

A Space Age Scandal in the Church
Would Aliens Be Welcome?
By Francis DeBernardo, New Ways Ministry

ACCORDING to the New Ways Ministry a space age scandal is brewing in Rome. In a recent editorial the ministry asked if there were any lessons to be learned from accounts of space aliens and exorcisms in the church.

The blog gave its opinion thusly:

Space aliens made headlines because of Pope Francis' well-noted line that if Martians showed up on earth and asked to be baptized, he would do so. Out of context, the statement sounds extremely bizarre, but in the context of the homily he was giving, the pope's comments make some sense. He was trying to make the point that the Spirit of God, not our human prejudices, should lead us to act. Catholic News Service provided context for the pope's remarks, which were given in a homily on Acts 11:1-18:

"From the very beginnings of Christianity, the pope said, church leaders and members have been tempted at times to block the Holy Spirit's path or try to control it.

" 'When the Lord shows us the way, who are we to say, "No, Lord, it is not prudent! No, let's do it this way" he said. 'Who are we to close doors?'

"Many parishes, Pope Francis said, have ushers to open the church doors and welcome people in, 'but there has never been a ministry for those who close the doors. Never.' "

Francis is not the first Vatican insider to toy with the idea of alien life. In 2008, Father Jose Gabriel Funes, director of the Vatican Observatory, told *L'Osservatore Romano* that "believing in the possible existence of extraterrestrial life is not opposed to Catholic doctrine" in an article entitled "The Alien is my Brother."

He said that since astronomers—even Catholic ones—believe that the universe is made up of 100 billion galaxies, so it is not reasonable to discount that some could have planets. "How could it not be left out that life developed elsewhere?" he pondered in the article. "As a multiplicity of creatures exist on earth, so there could be other beings, also intelligent, created by God. This does not contrast with our faith because we cannot put limits on the creative freedom of God. [According to] Saint Francis, if we consider earthly creatures as 'brother' and 'sister,' why cannot we also speak of an 'extraterrestrial brother'? It would therefore be a part of creation."

Funes' views were backed up in 2010, when fellow Vatican Observatory astronomer and Jesuit Brother Guy Consolmagno penned the book ***Intelligent Life in the Universe? Catholic Belief and the Search for Extraterrestrial Intelligent Life***. In it, he posed a number of questions, including whether aliens exist, and if they do and have souls, could they be baptized?

The answer, apparently, is yes. "The limitless universe might even include other planets with other beings created by that same loving God," he wrote in the book. "The idea of there being other races and other intelligences is not contrary to traditional Christian thought. There is nothing in Holy Scripture that could confirm or contradict the possibility of intelligent life elsewhere in the universe."

When *Gay Star News* ran the story about aliens, they did so with the headline: "Pope Francis will not marry gay couples, but will baptize aliens." While that is true enough, it is a little misleading, too, since the pope did not make any comment at the time about marrying gay couples. Moreover, the Gay Star News story doesn't even mention marriage in the body of the text.

But more importantly, it misses the point that Pope Francis' message was actually a message of welcome, of saying the church is open for all, even those who we might think of as the most "alien" to ourselves. To me, that is a wonderful message of welcome to Catholics who feel marginalized, such as many LGBT Catholics do.

What is also wonderful about this story is that Pope Francis' question, "Who are we to close doors?" so beautifully echoes his famous comments about gay priests, "Who am I to judge?" It seems that Pope Francis is building up a theme in his pontificate of cautioning people from feeling too arrogant.

The news stories about the exorcisms might be a little more complicated. *The Washington Post* ran a story about Pope Francis' seeming interest in the reality of the devil and the rite of exorcism. Entitled "A modern pope gets old school on the Devil," the article notes:

"After his little more than a year atop the Throne of St. Peter, Francis's teachings on Satan are already regarded as the most old school of any pope since at least Paul VI, whose papacy in the 1960s and 1970s fully embraced the notion of hellish forces plotting to deliver mankind unto damnation.

"Largely under the radar, theologians and Vatican insiders say, Francis has not only dwelled far more on Satan in sermons and speeches than his recent predecessors have, but also sought to rekindle the Devil's image as a supernatural entity with the forces of evil at his beck and call."

The article explores Catholic history and ideas about the devil, but where the topic becomes problematic for Catholic LGBT advocates is when it quotes a priest who is a practicing Catholic exorcist and an experience he had on an airplane:

". . . [T]he Rev. Cesar Truqui, an exorcist based in Switzerland, recounted one experience he had aboard a Swissair flight. 'Two lesbians,' he said, had sat behind him on the plane. Soon afterward, he said, he felt Satan's presence. As he silently sought to repel the evil spirit through prayer, one of the women, he said, began growling demonically and threw chocolates at his head.

"Asked how he knew the woman was possessed, he said that 'once you hear a Satanic growl, you never forget it. It's like smelling Margherita pizza for the first time. It's something you never forget.' "

The homophobia in such a comment makes one realize that so much of "devil talk" relies more on people's own prejudices, and less on a belief in objective evil.

It's not just Catholicism that runs this risk of prejudicial Satan-labeling when it comes to lesbian and gay people. Certain Charismatic Christian groups are also involved in such activity. Slate.com's Mark Joseph Stern wrote an article that took a look "Inside The Horrifying World of Gay Exorcisms." He cites a very reliable source, credible because he experienced such an exorcism:

"Roland Stringfellow, a pastor of the gay-friendly Metropolitan Community Church of Detroit, notes that these denominations spiritualize just about everything and believe that people have a spirit for every problem. Homosexuality, to these religions, is its own discrete problem-one even more troubling than alcoholism or drug addiction. Accordingly, Charismatic congregations are eager to cast the 'demon' of homosexuality out of gay people through exorcism, often in public at the altar of a church.

"Stringfellow himself was subject to such an exorcism when he was in college and was still closeted.

"'I was trying to get rid of my same-sex attractions,' he told me. 'The person at the altar yelled so everyone could hear: "Demon of homosexuality! Come out of this young man!" And he smacked me on my forehead to "slay me in the spirit."A friend had to get me up from the altar, pick me up, and get me back to my seat, because I was absolutely mortified. My secret had now been announced, proclaimed, to all of these individuals.' "

Professor Mathew Schmalz, College of the Holy Cross, a Jesuit school, acknowledges a belief in the reality of the Devil, but he notes that the recent rise of interest in Satan can be dangerous. Schmalz concludes a Huffington Post article on the topic with the following concluding paragraph:

"As a Catholic, I do believe that Satan exists and that there is something both intellectually and psychologically valuable in understanding evil as an objective force or entity. But I was also always taught that Lucifer was the most beautiful of the angels - and that evil can come under the most beguiling and attractive forms. For this reason, we have to be very careful where we see the Devil. When you try to cast out demons, it's all too easy to conjure more in the process."

Schmalz' caution is one that U.S. Catholic bishops should heed, especially when they ramp up their rhetoric, a la Springfield, Illinois Bishop Thomas Paprocki, to insinuate that marriage equality is the work of the devil.

The Roman Catholic Church's relationship with science has come a long way since Galileo was tried as a heretic in 1633 and forced to recant his finding that the Earth revolves around the sun. Church teaching at the time placed Earth at the center of the universe.

Today top clergy openly endorse scientific ideas like the Big Bang theory as a reasonable explanation for the creation of the universe. The theory says the universe began billions of years ago in the explosion of a single, super-dense point that contained all matter.

In 2009, the Vatican also sponsored a conference on evolution to mark the 150th anniversary of Charles Darwin's "The Origin of Species."

The event snubbed proponents of alternative theories, like creationism and intelligent design, which see a higher being rather than the undirected process of natural selection behind the evolution of species.

Still, there are divisions on the issues within the Catholic Church and within other religions, with some favoring creationism or intelligent design that could make it difficult to accept the concept of alien life.

Working with scientists to explore fundamental questions that are of interest to religion is in line with the teachings of Pope Benedict XVI, who has made strengthening the relationship between faith and reason a key aspect of his papacy.

Recent popes have been working to overcome the accusation that the church was hostile to science - a reputation grounded in the Galileo affair.

In 1992, Pope John Paul II declared the ruling against the astronomer was an error resulting from "tragic mutual incomprehension."

The Vatican Museums opened an exhibit marking the 400th anniversary of Galileo's first celestial observations. Tommaso Maccacaro, president of Italy's national institute of astrophysics, said at the exhibit's Oct. 13 opening that astronomy has had a major impact on the way we perceive ourselves.

"It was astronomical observations that let us understand that Earth (and man) don't have a privileged position or role in the universe," he said. "I ask myself what tools will we use in the next 400 years, and I ask what revolutions of understanding they'll bring about, like resolving the mystery of our apparent cosmic solitude."

The Vatican Observatory has also been at the forefront of efforts to bridge the gap between religion and science. Its scientist-clerics have generated top-notch research and its meteorite collection is considered one of the world's best. The observatory, founded by Pope Leo XIII in 1891, is based in Castel Gandolfo, a lakeside town in the hills outside Rome where the pope has his summer residence. It also conducts research at an observatory at the University of Arizona, in Tucson.

Insiders Claim Satanists In Control of the Vatican

"Through some crack or other in the temple of God, the smoke of Satan has entered." — **Pope Paul VI, 1972**

A book published by a retired priest, Msgr. Luigi Marinelli, has caused a lot of controversy in Italy. Gone With the Wind at the Vatican flew off the shelves as Italians eagerly consumed its stories of greedy bishops, money-laundering prelates, and even sexual abuse. In so doing, he became but the latest Vatican insider to allege that satanic rituals have been performed within the walls of the Holy See. Another recent book, the anonymously written Blood Lies in the Vatican, also hinted at Masonic plots in Rome.

This latest round began with allegations described as "explosive," made in Rome in November 1996 by an archbishop that members of the Roman Catholic hierarchy there are secretly involved in formal satanic worship. These charges have been confirmed as true by a well-known Vatican insider and are all the more remarkable by the total lack of notice in the US press.

Archbishop Emmanuel Milingo, 71, is a formerly high-ranking cleric who first spoke out about Satanism in the Vatican, and took a lot of heat for it.

Recently, Cardinal Joseph Ratzinger, the Vatican's chief doctinal enforcer, has banned charismatic healing sessions and exorcisms during Mass. In particular, a diocesan bishop can now forbid another bishop from conducting exorcisms in his diocese — a direct slap at Milingo, who as an archbishop, has been able to conduct his wildly popular healing sessions wherever he wanted. This has angered the Vatican, which recently removed him from his post as Special Delegate for the Pontifical Council for Migrants, rendering him unimportant to the Curia.

He had already been exiled some three years ago when his exuberant rites, characterized by some ecclesiastics of owing more to traditional African witchcraft than Catholicism, attracted too much attention. "Tales of [his] miraculous cures from cancer, AIDS and other terminal illnesses abound in Italy.

Thousands converge on his services to witness people, reputedly possessed with demons, writhing in agony on the floor while Milingo conducts his mass exorcism - dancing, singing and shouting." (London Telegraph, 2/7/99)

He has also made enemies of his fellow Zambian priests, who accused him of practicing "black magic" — as he has accused an unidentified cabal of Vatican clerics of doing. Subjected to a trial that he said resembled the Inquisition, he was cleared by the personal intervention of Pope John Paul II, who allegedly described him as a "lightning rod for the Devil." But Milingo was nevertheless stripped of his archbishop's rank.

This happened, ironically, around the time the Vatican decided to play down the existence of the Devil. Evil is now seen as a pervasive, deceptive force, rather than as a personal being which can possess humans. The new view emphasizes psychology, since according to Msgr. Corrado Balducci, a Vatican exorcist who recently declared that aliens are not devils either, most cases brought to the Church's attention come from psychiatric disturbances, not demons.

Perhaps, but in so doing, the new ritual seems to have been severely weakened. Pope John Paul II himself, along with his chief exorcist, were bested by the Devil during an attempted exorcism of a 15-year-old girl not long ago. Is it Vatican jealousy at work or is there another, more ominous reason? Could the very halls of the Holy See themselves have been infiltrated by Satanists as Milingo and others have asserted?

The Exorcist's Accusations

Milingo first made the accusations in an address to an audience of clergy and laity from across the globe at the Fatima 2000 International Congress on World Peace, held in Rome on November 18-23, 1996. Commenting on the growth of evil in the world and the need for more exorcists to aid the many people afflicted by demonic activity, he stated:

Now the third dimension [of evil] is the most dangerous. It is subtle and most terrible. . . I could not believe when I discovered this third dimension of evil. The third dimension is people who follow instructions in satanic sects. . .

Now with this third dimension, I'm sorry to say, our Church belongs to it. I'm very sorry, I could not understand myself, and even now I don't understand.

But the only consolation I have is that, well, Judas Iscariot was one. Together with Jesus for three years, he never changed, then I understand that the third dimension of evil existed not only now, but it existed even then. Because nothing could change the heart of Judas Iscariot — nothing. (Emphasis added.)

Milingo, formerly Archbishop of Lusaka, Zambia, has written books such as Face to Face With the Devil, and travels around the world preaching and healing. He has publicly accused fellow Catholic clergymen of harboring Satan's minions:

The devil in the Catholic Church is so protected now that he is like an animal protected by the government; put on a game preserve that outlaws anyone, especially hunters, from trying to capture or kill it. The devil within the Church today is actually protected by certain Church authorities from the official devil-hunter in the Church — the exorcist. So much so that the exorcist today is forbidden to attack the devil. The devil is so protected that the one who is the hunter, the exorcist, is forbidden to do his job.

Statements like these understandably caused a furor in the Italian press, gaining front-page headlines. Three days after his speech Milingo gave a press conference to clarify his remarks, causing a second outburst of sensational media coverage. To the question, "Are there men of the Curia who are followers of Satan?" the prelate replied, "Certainly there are priests and bishops. I stop at this level of ecclesiastical hierarchy because I am an archbishop, higher than this I cannot go."

It should be noted that the only ranks higher than archbishop in the Roman Catholic Church are those of the cardinals and the Pope himself.

Il Tempo and other major daily papers reported that Milingo used a statement by Pope Paul VI to back up his charges. In 1972, Paul surveyed the wreckage to the Church after the Second Vatican Council and was widely reported to have said, "From somewhere or other, the smoke of Satan has entered the temple of God." Milingo added, "I have not heard that anyone has seen him leave. We must pray that he will go away."

Nary a word of this made it into the American media, until it was reported in the Winter 1997 issue of The Fatima Crusader, a conservative pro-Marian Catholic newsletter associated with the group that sponsored the Fatima 2000 Congress. The story was picked up by William F. Jasper and reported in The New American, the organ of the John Birch Society, a right-wing political group, in the issue of March 3, 1997.

Milingo's remarks have been strangely ignored by the American press. The New American claimed that a Lexis/Nexis data search found not a single mention of his Fatima 2000 Congress statements, and were informed by an Associated Press researcher that Milingo was considered "a big old mouth" that was always spouting "a lot of insanity," because of his outspoken opinions about such things as the existence of Satan and of miracles.

A Sudden Defection

Then recently, to the undoubted shock of his followers and the delight of his enemies, Milingo has, to all intents, jumped ship. On Sunday, May 27, 2001, the controversial archbishop married a Korean acupuncturist, Maria Sung, 43. The woman was chosen for him, and the ceremony was presided over, by none other than the Rev. Sun Myung Moon, head of the Unification Church and self-proclaimed Messiah.

Automatic excommunication should be the result if the Vatican considers him guilty of apostasy or violating the Church's celibacy laws. Roman Catholic canon law, of course, frowns on marriages by senior clerics, no matter who does the ceremony.

After the wedding, conducted by Moon in a ballroom at the New York Hilton with about 60 other couples, Milingo told reporters the Vatican's threat of excommunication meant "nothing" to him. "It doesn't affect me," he declared. "I have an obligation to carry out what the Lord wants, and that's what I'm doing."

"God is still with me," he said. "I love my church." In a later statement, he said he and his new bride would return to Africa to bring a mission of healing to the AIDS and war-ravaged continent.

The archbishop was not the only renegade cleric to wed that day. Former Roman Catholic priest George Stallings, 53, now archbishop of his own breakaway African American church, also wed, as did numerous Christians and Muslims.

The Vatican was indeed swift to react. The very next day, chief spokesman Joaquin Navarro-Valls said that Milingo "could not be considered a bishop of the

Catholic Church" and would be subject to "foreseen canonical sanctions." This almost certainly means formal excommunication.

Milingo's decision to marry is viewed as a slap in the face for Pope John Paul II, who had shown him leniency despite pressure from leading Vatican officials. Senior Roman Catholic church sources said the Zambian bishops would ask the Vatican to expedite the excommunication of Milingo from the Church for what they saw as a betrayal.

"Milingo has betrayed the Zambian people and the Catholic Church. If it is in the name of Jesus and the glory of God he acted, then it is incomprehensible that he was married by a man whose followers consider (him) the messiah," one source told Reuters.

Incredibly, the Unification Church has been linked to devil worship in Zambia and has been forced to clear its name in the courts.

According to some experts, Moon, facing a steady loss in his ranks, looks to Africa as a new recruiting ground. Undoubtedly, the acquisition of such a charismatic figure as Milingo is quite a feather in his crown.

The effect of this on Milingo's followers, including those in the Fatima movement, is bound to be catastrophic. In one move, he has done to himself what his enemies in the Curia could not accomplish in twenty years. And in so doing, he has unfortunately lost much of whatever credibility he may have had.

Not long after his marriage, Milingo returned the Church. It was reported that after a retreat he had reconciled with the Pope and renounced his wedding. His new wife said she would launch a hunger strike in protest. Not much has been heard since and it is doubtful Milingo will ever speak out again.

Another Exorcist

In The Fatima Crusader article, Malachi Martin, a scholar, Vatican insider, and best-selling author, said, "Archbishop Milingo is a good bishop and his contention that there are Satanists in Rome is completely correct. Anybody who is acquainted with the state of affairs in the Vatican in the last 35 years is well aware that the prince of darkness has had and still has his surrogates in the court of St. Peter in Rome."

He said more members of the clergy becoming aware of the situation, and that Archbishop Milingo was "merely like that actor in the movie Network, who got fed up and said, 'I'm not going to take it anymore.'"

But Martin had his own allegations of Vatican skullduggery to make, ones that were much more detailed and serious than those of Milingo. These will be discussed in detail in the next article.

The relic was in his backpack, which was swiped by thieves but later recovered in a thicket of cane grass by police.

Chief Exorcist Says Devil is in Vatican

Father Gabriele Amorth in 2010 said people who are possessed by Satan vomit shards of glass and pieces of iron. He added that the assault on Pope Benedict XVI on Christmas Eve 2009 by a mentally unstable woman and the sex abuse scandals which have engulfed the Church in the U.S., Ireland, Germany and other countries, were proof that the Anti-Christ was waging a war against the Holy See.

"The Devil resides in the Vatican and you can see the consequences," said Father Amorth, 85, who has been the Holy See's chief exorcist for 25 years.

"He can remain hidden, or speak in different languages, or even appear to be sympathetic. At times he makes fun of me. But I'm a man who is happy in his work."

While there was "resistance and mistrust" towards the concept of exorcism among some Catholics, Pope Benedict XVI has no such doubts, Father Amorth said. "His Holiness believes wholeheartedly in the practice of exorcism. He has encouraged and praised our work," he added.

The evil influence of Satan was evident in the highest ranks of the Catholic hierarchy, with "cardinals who do not believe in Jesus and bishops who are linked to the demon," Father Amorth said.

In a rare insight into the world of exorcism, the Italian priest told *La Repubblica* newspaper that the 1973 film The Exorcist gave a "substantially exact" impression of what it was like to be possessed by the Devil.

People possessed by evil sometimes had to be physically restrained by half a dozen people while they were exorcised. They would scream, utter blasphemies and spit out sharp objects, he said.

"From their mouths, anything can come out – pieces of iron as long as a finger, but also rose petals," said Father Amorth, who claims to have performed 70,000 exorcisms. "When the possessed dribble and slobber, and need cleaning up, I do that too. Seeing people vomit doesn't bother me. The exorcist has one principal duty - to free human beings from the fear of the Devil."

The attempted assassination of Pope John Paul II by a Turkish gunman in 1981 and recent revelations of "violence and paedophilia" committed by Catholic priests against children in their care was also the work of the Devil, said Father Amorth, who has written a book about his vocation, Memoirs of an Exorcist, which was published recently.

Father Amorth, who is the president of the Association of Exorcists and fought as a partisan during the war, has previously claimed that both Hitler and Stalin were possessed by the Devil.

In an interview with Vatican Radio in 2006, he said: "Of course the Devil exists and he can not only possess a single person but also groups and entire populations.

"I am convinced that the Nazis were all possessed. All you have to do is think about what Hitler and Stalin did."

He also condemned the Harry Potter books, saying they were dangerous because they dabbled in the occult and failed to draw a clear distinction between "the Satanic art" of black magic and benevolent white magic.

Amorth authored two books specifically on exorcism. The two books *An Exorcist Tells His Story* and *An Exorcist: More Stories* are not official Roman Catholic documents, rather personal accounts of his office as Exorcist. The books use witness accounts and personal experience as evidence. The two books include references to official Roman Catholic teachings on demonology, however the main emphasis is on Amorth's experience as an exorcist. Both include references to the diagnosis and treatment of spiritual problems.

The books briefly cover the topics of demonic contraction and curses. On curses he states that, "A curse can originate from such things as maledictions by close relatives, a habit of blaspheming, membership in Freemasonry, spiritic or magic practices, and so on."

Amorth was also interviewed for the second episode of True Horror with Anthony Head, presented by Anthony Head. He stated that he never performs exorcisms on people who claim they are possessed without being so, and that he always sends people to see psychiatrists and psychologists before coming to him, and even mentioned an anecdote: that when he sees someone is not possessed but the person insists, he replies: "You have no Devil. If you have a problem, talk to a good vet."

Schoolgirl Kidnapped For Vatican Sex Parties

Father Amorth has also claimed that a 15-year-old Italian schoolgirl, Emanuela Orlandi, who was a citizen of Vatican City, was kidnapped for sex parties by a gang involving Vatican police and foreign diplomats. He said the girl was snatched from the streets of central Rome in June of 1983 and forced to take part in sex parties.

"This was a crime with a sexual motive. Parties were organized, with a Vatican gendarme acting as the 'recruiter' of the girls.

"The network involved diplomatic personnel from a foreign embassy to the Holy See. I believe Emanuela ended up a victim of this circle," Father Amorth, the honorary president of the International Association of Exorcists, told La Stampa newspaper.

Orlandi was in her second year at a liceo scientifico (a scientific high school) in Rome. Although the school year had concluded, she continued to take flute lessons three times per week at the Tommaso Ludovico Da Victoria School, connected with the Pontificium Institutum Musicæ Sacræ (The Pontifical Institute of Sacred Music). She was also part of the choir of Saint Anne's Church. Orlandi, the daughter of a Vatican bank employee who lived with her family inside Vatican City, just across the river from the Basilica, was the fourth of Ercole and Maria Orlandi's five children.

Emanuela usually travelled by bus to the music school. She would get off the bus after a few stops and then walk six or seven hundred feet. On June 22, 1983, Emanuela was late to class. She later explained her tardiness in a phone call to her sister, during which she said she had a job offer from a representative of Avon Cosmetics. Her sister suggested she talk it over with their parents before making any decisions. Emanuela allegedly met with the Avon rep shortly before her music lesson. At the end of the lesson, Emanuela spoke of the job offer with a girlfriend, who then left the girl at a bus stop in the company of another girl. Emanuela was allegedly last seen getting into a large, dark-colored BMW.

The debate over who kidnapped Emanuela and what became of her has raged in Italy for three decades. It has been suggested that she was taken by the leader of a notorious gang of criminals, who wanted to put pressure on Vatican officials to recover money that he had allegedly lent them.

Another theory is that she was abducted to be used as a bargaining chip for the release from prison of Mehmet Ali Agca, the Turkish gunman who tried to kill John Paul II in St Peter's Square in 1981, reportedly on the orders of the KGB. However, Father Amorth, 85, dismissed the "international dimension", saying that a Vatican archivist had also come to the conclusion that Emanuela was abducted for sexual exploitation.

In 2012 investigators opened the tomb of Enrico "Renatino" De Pedis, the gang leader, in order to check long-standing claims that the remains of the teenager were buried alongside him. They found his remains inside the tomb in the Sant' Apollinare basilica in Rome and also, intriguingly, other bones in a crypt nearby. However, those bones have never been positively identified as Emanuela's.

Emanuela's brother, Pietro Orlandi asked Pope Francis in 2013 to release tape recordings of to the courts of negotiations that went on between the Holy See and the possible kidnappers.

Orlandi wants answers to one aspect of the case in particular. Marco Fassoni Accetti was the key witness in the disappearance, who helped find the flute Emanuela allegedly had with her at the time. Accetti's confessor at the San Giuseppe De Merode College in Rome was Archbishop Pier Luigi Celata, currently the Vice Camerlengo of the Holy Roman Church and secretary of Agostino Casaroli (Vatican Secretary of State) at the time of Emanuela's disappearance, used to take the calls on a phone line coded 158. On July 17, 1983, a tape was found containing a recording of the Vatican and the kidnappers negotiating a swap: the girl, in exchange for Mehmet Ali Ağca, the man who tried to shoot Pope John Paul II. The alleged kidnappers also demanded a direct phone line to the Vatican Secretary of State, Casaroli. A girl could be heard moaning in the background, pleading for help and saying she did not feel well.

Some days later, the caller - nicknamed "The American" because of his strong American accent – rang again asking Emanuela's uncle to make the message recorded on the tape public and ask Cardinal Casaroli for information about a previous conversation. The American made 16 calls in total, all of them from public pay phones. Despite the various demands made and his claims of possessing proof, the man (who was never traced) did not provide clues that led anywhere.

The Orlandi family asked Pope Francis to hand all tape recordings of the conversations over to the courts. The judges who were examining the case were never given the tapes.

"Although more than 30 years have gone by, the pain is just as strong as it was on the day of her disappearance," Pietro Orlandi said. "Unfortunately, 30 years on, we are still in the dark about what happened that evening, but we are not giving up, we are moving forward and thanks to the support shown by ordinary people, we as a family feel even more motivated to go on," he added. Pietro says behind his sister's disappearance "lies something else, something big, 30 years of omissions and diversions."

The Italian Insider ran a story on April 25, 2013 revealing that a self-styled secret agent who claimed he helped kidnap Vatican schoolgirl Emanuela Orlandi was convicted for killing in 1983 the son of a Uruguayan official at the UN food agency IFAD, police sources said.

Marco Fassino Accetti, 58, claimed he was part of an Italian secret service dirty tricks gang that kidnapped Emanuela and Mirella Gregori, another teenager who disappeared the same year, purportedly to put pressure on the Holy See. Accetti's account contained some contradictions but earned credibility when he disclosed to the television programme Chi l'ha Visto the whereabouts of the flute that Orlandi had with her when she was abducted.

Investigators had never made public that the flute was a Ramponi and Cazzani model she carried in a case lined in red velvet. Accetti produced a detailed map that allowed police to find the flute and its black case wrapped in newspapers from 1983. Accetti claims that both teenagers were persuaded to accept their abduction without the use of force and were eventually moved to Paris where he believes they are still alive. Other witnesses in the past claim that Emanuela was murdered by Enrico de Pedis, a charismatic mobster with links to secret services.

Journalists from Chi l'ha visto, a tv programme that specializes in tracing missing persons, disclosed that six months after the disappearance of Emanuela, Accetti was held for questioning by police in connection with the death of a 12-

year-old boy, Josè G., the son of a Uruguayan official working for the International Fund for Agriculture and Development, who disappeared on the evening of Dec. 20, 1983 in the EUR district of Rome.

The boy's body was found the next day at Castel Porziano near Ostia by a bus driver and Accetti was arrested on charges of running the boy over while driving a Ford van.

Investigators at the time suspected the boy may have been kidnapped, according to a report in *Il Fatto Quotidiano* newspaper, but were unable to prove it was anything other than an accident and Accetti in the end was convicted solely for manslaughter. It was unclear why anyone should want to abduct the boy though officials at the UN agencies in Rome often have been known to use jobs there to obtain quasi diplomatic cover for espionage activities.

Accetti claims he decided to disclose what he knows about Emanuela's kidnapping because of the new climate of openness at the Vatican with the election of Pope Francis. Forensic experts are carrying out tests on the flute to try and determine whether there are traces of saliva or fingerprints carrying Emanuela's DNA.

The Devil and the Pope

REPORTER Nicole Winfield writing for the Associated Press asks the burning question: Is Pope Francis an exorcist? Can he kick the devil to the curb? Is it possible for the leader of the Catholic Church to tell all manner of demon and evil spirit to be gone?

Says journalist Winfield: "Pope Francis' fascination with the devil took on remarkable new twists Tuesday, with a well-known exorcist insisting Francis helped "liberate" a Mexican man possessed by four different demons despite the Vatican's insistence that no such papal exorcism took place.

The case concerns a 43-year-old husband and father who traveled to Rome from Mexico to attend Francis' Mass on Sunday in St. Peter's Square. At the end of the Mass, Francis blessed several wheelchair-bound faithful as he always does, including a man possessed by the devil, according to the priest who brought him, the Rev. Juan Rivas."

This is how the AP report says it all went down: "Francis laid his hands on the man's head and recited a prayer. The man heaved deeply a half-dozen times, shook, then slumped in his wheelchair. The images, broadcast worldwide, prompted the television station of the Italian bishops' conference to declare that according to several exorcists, there was "no doubt" that Francis either performed an exorcism or a simpler prayer to free the man from the devil."

But Winfield says, "The Vatican was more cautious. In a statement Tuesday, it said Francis "didn't intend to perform any exorcism. But as he often does for the sick or suffering, he simply intended to pray for someone who was suffering who was presented to him."The Rev. Gabriele Amorth, a leading exorcist for the diocese of Rome, said he performed a lengthy exorcism of his own on the man Tuesday morning and ascertained he was possessed by four separate demons. The case was related to the legalization of abortion in Mexico City, he said. Amorth told RAI state radio that even a short prayer, without the full rite of exorcism being performed, is in itself a type of exorcism.

"That was a true exorcism," he said of Francis' prayer. "Exorcisms aren't just done according to the rules of the ritual.'"

As it stands, it was reported that, "Rivas took the Vatican line, saying it was no exorcism but that Francis merely said a prayer to free the man from the devil. 'Since no one heard what he said, including me who was right there, you can say he did a prayer for liberation but nothing more,' Rivas wrote on his Facebook page, which was confirmed by his religious order, the Legionaries of Christ.

Fueling the speculation that Francis did indeed perform an exorcism is his frequent reference to Satan in his homilies — as well as an apparent surge in demand for exorcisms among the faithful despite the irreverent treatment the rite often receives from Hollywood."

Winfield asks, "Who can forget the green vomit and the spinning head of the possessed girl in the 1973 cult classic "The Exorcist"? In his very first homily as pope on March 14, Francis warned cardinals gathered in the Sistine Chapel the day after he was elected that "he who doesn't pray to the Lord prays to the devil." The AP news story states that the Pope, " has since mentioned the devil on a handful of occasions, most recently in a May 4 homily when in his morning Mass in the Vatican hotel chapel he spoke of the need for dialogue — except with Satan. "With the prince of this world you can't have dialogue: Let this be clear!" he warned.

The article continues by noting that, "Experts said Francis' frequent invocation of the devil is a reflection both of his Jesuit spirituality and his Latin American roots, as well as a reflection of a Catholic Church weakened by secularization. "The devil's influence and presence in the world seems to fluctuate in quantity inversely proportionate to the presence of Christian faith," said the Rev. Robert Gahl, a moral theologian at Rome's Pontifical Holy Cross University. "So, one would expect an upswing in his malicious activity in the wake of de-Christianization and secularization" in the world and a surge in things like drug use, pornography and superstition."

"In recent years," states the piece, "Rome's pontifical universities have hosted several courses for would-be exorcists on the rite, updated in 1998 and contained in a little red leather-bound booklet. The rite is relatively brief, consisting of blessings with holy water, prayers and an interrogation of the devil in which the exorcist demands to know the devil's name, how many are present and when they will leave the victim."

Only a priest authorized by a bishop can perform an exorcism, and canon law specifies that the exorcist must be "endowed with piety, knowledge, prudence and integrity of life."

While belief in the devil is consistent with church teaching, the Holy See does urge prudence, particularly to ensure that the victim isn't merely psychologically ill.

The Rev. Giulio Maspero, a Rome-based systematic theologian who has witnessed or participated in more than a dozen exorcisms, says he's fairly certain that Francis' prayer on Sunday was either a full-fledged exorcism or a more simple prayer to "liberate" the young man from demonic possession.

He noted that the placement of the pope's hands on the man's head was the "typical position" for an exorcist to use.

"When you witness something like that — for me it was shocking — I could feel the power of prayer," he said in a phone interview, speaking of his own previous experiences.

The Vatican spokesman, the Rev. Federico Lombardi, sought to temper speculation that what occurred was a full-fledged exorcism. While he didn't deny it outright — he said Francis hadn't "intended" to perform one — he stressed that the intention of the person praying is quite important. Later, the director of TV2000, the television of the Italian bishops' conference, went on the air to apologize for the earlier report.

"I don't want to attribute to him a gesture that he didn't intend to perform," said the director, Dino Boffo. That said, Francis' actions and attitude toward the devil are not new: As archbishop of Buenos Aires, the former Cardinal Jorge Mario Bergoglio frequently spoke about the devil in our midst.

In the book "***Heaven and Earth***," Bergoglio devoted the second chapter to "The Devil" and said in no uncertain terms that he believes in the devil and that Satan's fruits are "destruction, division, hatred and calumny." "Perhaps its greatest success in these times has been to make us think that it doesn't exist, that everything can be traced to a purely human plan," he wrote.

Italian newspapers noted that the late Pope John Paul II performed an exorcism in 1982 — near the same spot where Francis prayed over the young disabled man Sunday.

Blood of Pope John Paul II Stolen in Possible Satanic Theft

A religious reliquary containing blood from the late Pope John Paul II has been stolen on January 27, 2014 from a remote mountain church in Italy, with speculation that a Satanic group could be behind the theft.

A team of around 50 Carabinieri police officers with sniffer dogs were on Monday searching for any trace of the reliquary, which was stolen from the Church of St Peter of Ienca in the Abruzzo mountains at the weekend.

The ornate gold object contains a fragment of material, stained with blood, which was purportedly taken from the clothing worn by John Paul II after he was shot during the failed attempt on his life in St Peter's Square in 1981.

It was donated to the church in May 2011 by Stanislaw Dzuwisz, a Polish cardinal and the Pope's former personal secretary.

The reliquary is one of just a handful in the world that contains the blood of the Polish pope, who died in 2005 and was succeeded by Benedict XVI.

It was stolen along with a cross from the church, which lies close to Gran Sasso, a 9,550ft- high mountain in the Apennines east of Rome.

The British newspaper *The Telegraph* reported that the theft was discovered on by a priest from the religious sanctuary, which is dedicated to the memory of John Paul II.

The Pope was very fond of the region and used to spend holidays there, walking, meditating and skiing at the nearby resort of Campo Imperatore.

It is also famous as the place where Benito Mussolini was interned after Italy swapped sides during the war, and from where he was rescued by a team of German paratroopers in Sept 1943 during a daring airborne raid.

"It's possible that there could be Satanic sects behind the theft of the reliquary," said Giovanni Panunzio, the national coordinator of an anti-occult group called Osservatorio Antiplagio.

"This period of the year is important in the Satanic calendar and culminates in the Satanic 'new year' on Feb 1. This sort of sacrilege often take place at this time of the year. We hope that the stolen items are recovered as quickly as possible."

The theft of the reliquary comes as the Vatican prepares to canonize John Paul II, along with another former Pope, John XXIII, at a ceremony on April 27.

At John Paul II's funeral in 2005, crowds of mourners cried "Santo Subito!" - "Sainthood now" - prompting the Vatican to speed up the Polish pontiff's path to canonization.

In Aug 2012, another relic containing a vial of the late Pope's blood was stolen from a Catholic priest while he was travelling on a train north of Rome.

Magic and Divination in the Church

From *THEOSOPHY*, Vol. 57, No. 1, November, 1968

IN what countries have "divine miracles" flourished most, been most frequent and most stupendous? Catholic Spain, and Pontifical Italy, beyond question. And which more than these two, has had access to ancient literature?

Spain was famous for her libraries; the Moors were celebrated for their profound learning in alchemy and other sciences. The Vatican is the storehouse of an immense number of ancient manuscripts. During the long interval of nearly 1,500 years they have been accumulating, from trial after trial, books and manuscripts confiscated from their sentenced victims, to their own profit.

The Catholics may plead that the books were generally committed to the flames; that the treatises of famous sorcerers and enchanters perished with their accursed authors. But the Vatican, if it could speak, could tell a different story. It knows too well of the existence of certain closets and rooms, access to which is had but by the very few. It knows that the entrances to these secret hiding-places are so cleverly concealed from sight in the carved frame-work and under the profuse ornamentation of the library-walls, that there have even been Popes who lived and died within the precincts of the palace without ever suspecting their existence.

When one has such treasures at hand -- original manuscripts, papyri, and books pillaged from the richest libraries; old treatises on magic and alchemy; and records of all the trials for witchcraft, and sentences for the same to rack, stake, and torture, it is mighty easy to write volumes of accusations against the Devil. We affirm on good grounds that there are hundreds of the most valuable works on the occult sciences, which are sentenced to eternal concealment from the public, but are attentively read and studied by the privileged who have access to the Vatican Library.

In no Pagan temple was black magic, in its real and true sense, more practiced than in the Vatican. While strongly supporting exorcism as an important source of revenue, they neglected magic as little as the ancient heathen. It is easy to prove that the sortilegium, or sorcery, was widely practiced among the clergy and monks so late as the last century, and is practiced occasionally even now.

Where, in the records of European Magic, can we find cleverer enchanters than in the mysterious solitudes of the cloister? Albert Magnus, the famous Bishop and conjurer of Ratisbon, was never surpassed in his art. Roger Bacon was a monk, and Thomas Aquinas one of the most learned pupils of Albertus.

Trithemius, Abbot of the Spanheim Benedictines, was the teacher, friend, and confidant of Cornelius Agrippa; and while the confederations of the Theosophists were scattered broadcast about Germany, where they first originated, assisting one another, and struggling for years for the acquirement of esoteric knowledge, any person who knew how to become the favored pupil of certain monks, might very soon be proficient in all the important branches of occult learning.

This is all in history and cannot be easily denied. Magic, in all its aspects, was widely and nearly openly practiced by the clergy till the Reformation. And even he who was once called the "Father of the Reformation," the famous John Reuchlin, author of the Mirific Word and friend of Pico di Mirandola, the teacher and instructor of Erasmus, Luther, and Melancthon, was a kabalist and occultist.

The ancient Sortilegium, or divination by means of Sortes or lots – an art and practice now decried by the clergy as an abomination, designated by Stat. 10 Jac. as felony, and by Stat. 12 Carolus II. excepted out of the general pardons, on the ground of being sorcery – was widely practiced by the clergy and monks. In fact, it was sanctioned by St. Augustine himself, who does not "disapprove of this method of learning futurity, provided it be not used for worldly purposes." More than that, he confesses having practiced it himself.

The clergy called it Sortes Sanctorum, when it was they who practiced it; while the Sortes Prœnestinœ, succeeded by the Sortes Homericœ and Sortes Virgilianœ, were abominable heathenism, the worship of the Devil, when used by anyone else.

We must not forget that the Christian Church owes its present canonical Gospels, and hence its whole religious dogmatism, to the Sortes Sanctorum. Unable to agree as to which were the most divinely-inspired of the numerous gospels extant in its time, the mysterious Council of Nicea concluded to leave the decision of the puzzling question to miraculous intervention. This Nicean Council may well be called mysterious. There was a mystery, first, in the mystical number of its 318 bishops, on which Barnabas (viii, 11, 12, 13) lays such a stress; added to this, there is no agreement among ancient writers as to the time and place of its assembly, nor even as to the bishop who presided. Notwithstanding the grandiloquent eulogium of Constantine, Sabinus, the Bishop of Heraclea, affirms that "except Constantine, the emperor, and Eusebius Pamphilus, these bishops were a set of illiterate, simple creatures, that understood nothing;" which is equivalent to saying that they were a set of fools.

Such was apparently the opinion entertained of them by Pappus, who tells us of the bit of magic resorted to to decide which were the true gospels. In his Synodicon to that Council Pappus says, having "promiscuously put all the books that were referred to the Council for determination under a communion-table in a church, they (the bishops) besought the Lord that the inspired writings might get upon the table, while the spurious ones remained underneath, and it happened accordingly." But we are not told who kept the keys of the council chamber over night.

On the authority of ecclesiastical eye-witnesses, therefore, we are at liberty to say that the Christian world owes its "Word of God" to a method of divination, for resorting to which the Church subsequently condemned unfortunate victims as conjurers, enchanters, magicians, witches, and vaticinators, and burnt them by thousands. In treating of this truly divine phenomenon of the self-sorting manuscripts, the Fathers of the Church say that God himself presides over the Sortes.

Augustine confessed that he himself used this sort of divination. But opinions, like revealed religions, are liable to change. That which for nearly fifteen hundred years was imposed on Christendom as a book, of which every word was written under the direct supervision of the Holy Ghost; of which not a syllable, nor a comma could be changed without sacrilege, is now being retranslated, revised, corrected, and clipped of whole verses, in some cases of entire chapters. And yet, as soon as the new edition is out, its doctors would have us accept it as a new "Revelation" of the nineteenth century, with the alternative of being held as an infidel. Thus, we see that, no more within than without its precincts, is the infallible Church to be trusted more than would be reasonably convenient.

The forefathers of our modern divines found authority for the Sortes in the verse (Prov. 16:33) where it is said: "The lot is cast into the lap, but the whole disposing thereof is of the Lord," and now, their direct heirs hold that "the whole disposing thereof is of the Devil." Perhaps, they are unconsciously beginning to endorse the doctrine of the Syrian Bardesanes, that the actions of God, as well as of man, are subject to necessity?

The magical achievements of the Bishop of Ratisbon and those of the "angelic doctor," Thomas Aquinas, are too well known to need repetition; but we may explain farther how the "illusions" of the former were produced. If the Catholic bishop was so clever in making people believe on a bitter winter night that they were enjoying the delights of a splendid summer day, and cause the icicles hanging from the boughs of the trees in the garden to seem like so many tropical fruits, the Hindu magicians also practice such biological powers unto this very day, and claim the assistance of neither god nor devil. Such "miracles" are all produced by the same human power that is inherent in every man, if he only knew how to develop it.

About the time of the Reformation, the study of alchemy and magic had become so prevalent among the clergy as to produce great scandal. Cardinal Wolsey was openly accused before the court and the privy-council of confederacy with a man named Wood, a sorcerer, who said that "My Lord Cardinale had suche a rynge that whatsomevere he askyd of the Kynges grace that he hadd yt:" adding that "Master Cromwell, when he ... was servaunt in my lord cardynales housse ... rede many bokes and specyally the boke of Salamon ... and studied mettells and what vertues they had after the canon of Salamon." This case, with several others equally curious, is to be found among the Cromwell papers in the Record Office of the Rolls House.

A priest named William Stapleton was arrested as a conjurer, during the reign of Henry VIII, and an account of his adventures is still preserved in the Rolls House records. The Sicilian priest whom Benvenuto Cellini calls a necromancer, became famous through his successful conjurations, and was never molested. The remarkable adventure of Cellini with him in the Colosseum, where the priest conjured up a whole host of devils, is well known to the reading public. The subsequent meeting of Cellini with his mistress, as predicted and brought about by the conjurer, at the precise time fixed by him, is to be considered, as a matter of course, a "curious coincidence."

In the latter part of the sixteenth century there was hardly a parish to be found in which the priests did not study magic and alchemy. The practice of exorcism to cast out devils "in imitation of Christ," who by the way never used exorcism at all, led the clergy to devote themselves openly to "sacred" magic in contradistinction to black art, of which latter crime were accused all those who were neither priests nor monks.

The occult knowledge gleaned by the Roman Church from the once fat fields of theurgy she sedulously guarded for her own use, and sent to the stake only those practitioners who "poached" on her lands of the Scientia Scientiarum, and those whose sins could not be concealed by the friar's frock. The proof of it lies in the records of history. "In the course only of fifteen years, between 1580 to 1595, and only in the single province of Lorraine, the President Remigius burned 900 witches," says Thomas Wright, in his **Sorcery and Magic**.

"Ecclesia non novit Sanguinem!" meekly repeated the scarlet-robed cardinals. And to avoid the spilling of blood which horrified them, they instituted the Holy Inquisition. If, as the occultists maintain, and science half confirms, our most trifling acts and thoughts are indelibly impressed upon the eternal mirror of the astral ether, there must be somewhere, in the boundless realm of the unseen universe, the imprint of a curious picture. It is that of a gorgeous standard waving in the heavenly breeze at the foot of the great "white throne" of the Almighty. On its crimson damask face a cross, symbol of "the Son God who died for mankind," with an olive branch on one side, and a sword, stained to the hilt with human gore, on the other. A legend selected from the Psalms emblazoned in golden letters, reading thus: "Exurge, Domine, et judica causam meam." For such appears the standard of the Inquisition, on a photograph in our possession, from an original procured at the Escurial of Madrid.

Under this Christian standard, in the brief space of fourteen years, Tomas de Torquemada, the confessor of Queen Isabella, burned over ten thousand persons, and sentenced to the torture eighty thousand more. Orobio, the well-known writer, who was detained so long in prison, and who hardly escaped the flames of the Inquisition, immortalized this institution in his works when once at liberty in Holland. He found no better argument against the Holy Church than to embrace the Judaic faith and submit even to circumcision.

"In the cathedral of Saragossa," says a writer on the Inquisition, "is the tomb of a famous inquisitor. Six pillars surround the tomb; to each is chained a Moor, as preparatory to being burned."

On this St. Foix ingenuously observes: "If ever the Jack Ketch of any country should be rich enough to have a splendid tomb, this might serve as an excellent model!"

To make it complete, however, the builders of the tomb ought not to have omitted a bas-relief of the famous horse which was burnt for sorcery and witchcraft. Granger tells the story, describing it as having occurred in his time. The poor animal "had been taught to tell the spots upon cards, and the hour of the day by the watch. Horse and owner were both indicted by the sacred office for dealing with the Devil, and both were burned, with a great ceremony of auto-da-fé, at Lisbon, in 1601, as wizards!"

This immortal institution of Christianity did not remain without its Dante to sing its praise. "Macedo, a Portuguese Jesuit," says the author of Demonologia, "has discovered the origin of the Inquisition, in the terrestrial Paradise, and presumes to allege that God was the first who began the functions of an inquisitor over Cain and the workmen of Babel!"

The medieval as well as the modern phenomena, manifested through laymen, whether produced through occult knowledge or happening independently, upset the claims of both the Catholic and Protestant Churches to divine miracles. In the face of reiterated and unimpeachable evidence it became impossible for the former to maintain successfully the assertion that seemingly miraculous manifestations by the "good angels" and God's direct intervention could be produced exclusively by her chosen ministers and holy saints. Neither could the Protestant well maintain on the same ground that miracles had ended with the apostolic ages. For, whether of the same nature or not, the modern phenomena claimed close kinship with the biblical ones.

The magnetists and healers of our century came into direct and open competition with the apostles. The Zouave Jacob, of France, had outrivaled the prophet Elijah in recalling to life persons who were seemingly dead; and Alexis, the somnambulist, mentioned by Mr. Wallace in his work, was, by his lucidity, putting to shame apostles, prophets, and the Sibyls of old.

Since the burning of the last witch, the great Revolution of France, so elaborately prepared by the league of the secret societies and their clever emissaries, had blown over Europe and awakened terror in the bosom of the clergy. It had, like a destroying hurricane, swept away in its course those best allies of the Church, the Roman Catholic aristocracy. A sure foundation was now laid for the right of individual opinion. The world was freed from ecclesiastical tyranny by opening an unobstructed path to Napoleon the Great, who had given the deathblow to the Inquisition. This great slaughter-house of the Christian Church – wherein she butchered, in the name of the Lamb, all the sheep arbitrarily declared scurvy -- was in ruins, and she found herself left to her own responsibility and resources.

Peter and Paul

The majority of critics show that Peter never was at Rome at all; the reasons are many and unanswerable. Perhaps we had best begin by pointing to the works of Justin Martyr. This great champion of Christianity, writing in the early part of the second century in Rome, where he fixed his abode, eager to get hold of the least proof in favor of the truth for which he suffered, seems perfectly unconscious of St. Peter's existence. Neither does any other writer of any consequence mention him in connection with the Church of Rome, earlier than the days of Irenæus, when the latter set himself to invent a new religion, drawn from the depths of his imagination.

The very apostolic designation Peter is from the Mysteries. The Hierophant or supreme pontiff bore the title peter, or interpreter. The names Phtah, Peth'r, the residence of Balaam, Patara, and Patras, the names of oracle-cities, pateres or pateras and, perhaps, Buddha, all come from the same root. Jesus says: "Upon this petra I will build my Church, and the gates, or rulers of Hades, shall not prevail against it"; meaning by petra the rock-temple, and by metaphor, the Christian Mysteries; the adversaries to which were the old mystery-gods of the underworld, who were worshipped in the rites of Isis, Adonis, Atys, Sabazius, Dionysus, and the Eleusinia. No apostle Peter was ever at Rome; but the Pope, seizing the sceptre of the Pontifex Maximus, the keys of Janus and Kubelé, and adorning his Christian head with the cap of the Magna Mater, copied from that of the tiara of Brahmâtma, the Supreme Pontiff of the Initiates of old India, became the successor of the Pagan high priest, the real Peter-Roma, or Petroma.

The Roman Catholic Church has two far mightier enemies than the "heretics" and the "infidels"; and these are -- Comparative Mythology and Philology. There never was nor ever will be a truly philosophical mind, whether of Pagan, heathen, Jew, or Christian, but has followed the same path of thought. Gautama-Buddha is mirrored in the precepts of Christ; Paul and Philo Judæus are faithful echoes of Plato; and Ammonius Saccas and Plotinus won their immortal fame by combining the teachings of all these grand masters of true philosophy. "Prove all things; hold fast that which is good," ought to be the motto of all brothers on earth. Not so is it with the interpreters of the Bible. The seed of the Reformation was sown on the day that the second chapter of the Catholic Epistle of James, jostled the eleventh chapter of the Epistle to the Hebrews in the same New Testament. One who believes in Paul cannot believe in James, Peter, and John. The Paulists, to remain Christians with their apostle, must withstand Peter "to the face;" and if Peter "was to be blamed" and was wrong, then he was not infallible. How then can his successor boast of his infallibility? Every Kingdom divided against itself is brought to desolation; and every house divided against itself must fall. A plurality of masters has proved as fatal in religions as in politics.

What Paul preached was preached by every other mystic philosopher. "Stand fast therefore in the liberty wherewith Christ hath made us free, and be not entangled again with the yoke of bondage!" exclaims the honest apostle-philosopher; and adds, as if prophetically inspired: "But if ye bite and devour one another, take heed that ye be not consumed one of another."

For such men as Plotinus, Porphyry, Iamblichus, Apollonius, and even Simon Magus, to be accused of having formed a pact with the Devil, whether the latter personage exist or not, is so absurd as to need but little refutation. If Simon Magus – the most problematical of all in an historical sense – ever existed otherwise than in the overheated fancy of Peter and the other apostles, he was evidently no worse than any of his adversaries. A difference in religious views, however great, is insufficient per se to send one person to heaven and the other to hell. Such uncharitable and peremptory doctrine might have been taught in the middle ages; but it is too late now for even the Church to put forward this traditional scarecrow. Research begins to suggest that which, if ever verified, will bring eternal disgrace on the Church of the Apostle Peter, whose very imposition of herself upon that disciple must be regarded as the most unverified and unverifiable of the assumptions of the Catholic clergy.

The erudite author of Supernatural Religion assiduously endeavors to prove that by Simon Magus we must understand the apostle Paul, whose Epistles were secretly as well as openly calumniated by Peter, and charged with containing "dysnoëtic learning." The Apostle of the Gentiles was brave, outspoken, sincere, and very learned; the Apostle of Circumcision, cowardly, cautious, insincere, and very ignorant. That Paul had been, partially, at least, if not completely, initiated into the theurgic mysteries, admits of little doubt. His language, the phraseology so peculiar to the Greek philosophers, certain expressions used but by the initiates, are so many sure ear-marks to that supposition. Our suspicion has been strengthened by an article in one of the New

York periodicals, entitled *Paul and Plato*, in which the author puts forward one remarkable and, for us, very precious observation. In his Epistles to the Corinthians he shows Paul abounding with "expressions suggested by the initiations of Sabazius and Eleusis, and the lectures of the (Greek) philosophers. He (Paul) designates himself an idiotes – a person unskilful in the Word, but not in the gnosis or philosophical learning. 'We speak wisdom among the perfect or initiated,' he writes; 'not the wisdom of this world, nor of the archons of this world, but divine wisdom in a mystery, secret – which none of the Archons of this world knew.'"

What else can the apostle mean by these unequivocal words, but that he himself, as belonging to the mystœ (initiated), spoke of things shown and explained only in the Mysteries? The "divine wisdom in a mystery which none of the archons of this world knew," has evidently some direct reference to the basileus of the Eleusinian initiation who did know. The basileus belonged to the staff of the great hierophant, and was an archon of Athens; and as such was one of the chief mystœ, belonging to the interior Mysteries, to which a very select and small number obtained an entrance. The magistrates supervising the Eleusinians were called archons.

Another proof that Paul belonged to the circle of the "Initiates" lies in the following fact. The apostle had his head shorn at Cenchrea (where Lucius, Apuleius, was initiated) because "he had a vow." The nazars – or set apart – as we see in the Jewish Scriptures, had to cut their hair which they wore long, and which "no razor touched" at any other time, and sacrifice it on the altar of initiation. And the nazars were a class of Chaldean theurgists. We will show further that Jesus belonged to this class.

Paul declares that: "According to the grace of God which is given unto me, as a wise master-builder, I have laid the foundation."

This expression, master-builder, used only once in the whole Bible, and by Paul, may be considered as a whole revelation. In the Mysteries, the third part of the sacred rites was called Epopteia, or revelation, reception into the secrets. In substance it means that stage of divine clairvoyance when everything pertaining to this earth disappears, and earthly sight is paralyzed, and the soul is united free and pure with its Spirit, or God. But the real significance of the word is "overseeing," from optomai – I see myself. In Sanscrit the word evâpto has the same meaning, as well as to obtain. The word epopteia is a compound one, from Epi – upon, and optomai – to look, or an overseer, an inspector – also used for a master-builder. The title of master-mason, in Freemasonry, is derived from this, in the sense used in the Mysteries. Therefore, when Paul entitles himself a "master-builder," he is using a word pre-eminently kabalistic, theurgic, and masonic, and one which no other apostle uses. He thus declares himself an adept, having the right to initiate others.

If we search in this direction, with those sure guides, the Grecian Mysteries and the Kabala, before us, it will be easy to find the secret reason why Paul was so persecuted and hated by Peter, John, and James. The author of the Revelation was a Jewish kabalist pur sang, with all the hatred inherited by him from his forefathers toward the Mysteries. His jealousy during the life of Jesus extended even to Peter; and it is but after the death of their common master that we see the two apostles – the former of whom wore the Mitre and the Petaloon of the Jewish Rabbis – preach so zealously the rite of circumcision. In the eyes of Peter, Paul, who had humiliated him, and whom he felt so much his superior in "Greek learning" and philosophy, must have naturally appeared as a magician, a man polluted with the "Gnosis," with the "wisdom" of the Greek Mysteries – hence, perhaps, "Simon the Magician."

As to Peter, biblical criticism has shown before now that he had probably no more to do with the foundation of the Latin Church at Rome, than to furnish the pretext so readily seized upon by the cunning Irenæus to benefit this Church with the new name of the apostle – Petra or Kiffa, a name which allowed so readily, by an easy play upon words, to connect it with Petroma, the double set of stone tablets used by the hierophant at the initiation, during the final Mystery. In this, perhaps, lies concealed the whole secret of the claims of the Vatican. As Professor Wilder happily suggests: "In the Oriental countries the designation Peter (in Phoenician and Chaldaic, an interpreter) appears to have been the title of this personage (the hierophant)... There is in these facts some reminder of the peculiar circumstances of the Mosaic Law ... and also of the claim of the Pope to be the successor of Peter, the hierophant or interpreter of the Christian religion."

As such, we must concede to him, to some extent, the right to be such an interpreter. The Latin Church has faithfully preserved in symbols, rites, ceremonies, architecture, and even in the very dress of her clergy, the tradition of the Pagan worship -- of the public or exoteric ceremonies, we should add; otherwise her dogmas would embody more sense and contain less blasphemy against the majesty of the Supreme and Invisible God.

An inscription found on the coffin of Queen Mentuhept, of the eleventh dynasty (2250 B.C.), now proved to have been transcribed from the seventeenth chapter of the Book of the Dead (dating not later than 4500 B.C.), is more than suggestive. This monumental text contains a group of hieroglyphics, which, when interpreted, read thus:

PTR. Peter-   RF. ref-   SU. su.

Baron Bunsen shows this sacred formulary mixed up with a whole series of glosses and various interpretations on a monument forty centuries old. "This is identical with saying that the record (the true interpretation) was at that time no longer intelligible.... We beg our readers to understand," he adds, "that a sacred text, a hymn, containing the words of a departed spirit, existed in such a state about 4,000 years ago ... as to be all but unintelligible to royal scribes."

That it was unintelligible to the uninitiated among the latter is as well proved by the confused and contradictory glossaries, as that it was a "mystery"-word, known to the hierophants of the sanctuaries, and, moreover, a word chosen by Jesus, to designate the office assigned by him to one of his apostles. This word, PTR, was partially interpreted, owing to another word similarly written in another group of hieroglyphics, on a stele, the sign used for it being an opened eye.

Bunsen mentions as another explanation of PTR – "to show." "It appears to me," he remarks, "that our PTR is literally the old Aramaic and Hebrew 'Patar,' which occurs in the history of Joseph as the specific word for interpreting; whence also Pitrum is the term for interpretation of a text, a dream."

In a manuscript of the first century, a combination of the Demotic and Greek texts, and most probably one of the few which miraculously escaped the Christian vandalism of the second and third centuries, when all such precious manuscripts were burned as magical, we find occurring in several places a phrase, which, perhaps, may throw some light upon this question. One of the principal heroes of the manuscript, who is constantly referred to as "the Judean Illuminator" or Initiate, is made to communicate but with his Patar; the latter being written in Chaldaic characters. Once the latter word is coupled with the name Shimeon. Several times, the "Illuminator," who rarely breaks his contemplative solitude, is shown inhabiting a cave, and teaching the multitude of eager scholars standing outside, not orally, but through this Patar. The latter receives the words of wisdom by applying his ear to a circular hole in a partition which conceals the teacher from the listeners, and then conveys them, with explanations and glossaries, to the crowd. This, with a slight change, was the method used by Pythagoras, who, as we know, never allowed his neophytes to see him during the years of probation, but instructed them from behind a curtain in his cave.

But, whether the "Illuminator" of the Græco-Demotic manuscript is identical with Jesus or not, the fact remains, that we find him selecting a "mystery"-appellation for one who is made to appear later by the Catholic Church as the janitor of the Kingdom of Heaven and the interpreter of Christ's will. The word Patar or Peter locates both master and disciple in the circle of initiation, and connects them with the "Secret Doctrine." The great hierophant of the ancient Mysteries never allowed the candidates to see or hear him personally. He was the Deus-ex-Machina, the presiding but invisible Deity, uttering his will and instructions through a second party; and 2,000 years later, we discover that the Dalaï-Lamas of Thibet had been following for centuries the same traditional program during the most important religious mysteries of lamaism.

If Jesus knew the secret meaning of the title bestowed by him on Simon, then he must have been initiated; otherwise he could not have learned it; and if he was an initiate of either the Pythagorean Essenes, the Chaldean Magi, or the Egyptian Priests, then the doctrine taught by him was but a portion of the "Secret Doctrine" taught by the Pagan hierophants to the few selected adepts admitted within the sacred adyta.

We must once more return to that greatest of all the Patristic frauds; the one which has undeniably helped the Roman Catholic Church to its unmerited supremacy, viz.: the barefaced assertion, in the teeth of historical evidence, that Peter suffered martyrdom at Rome. It is but too natural that the Latin clergy should cling to it, for, with the exposure of the fraudulent nature of this pretext, the dogma of apostolic succession must fall to the ground.

There have been many able works of late, in refutation of this preposterous claim. Among others we note Mr. G. Reber's, ***The Christ of Paul***, which overthrows it quite ingeniously. The author proves, 1, that there was no church established at Rome, until the reign of Antoninus Pius; 2, that as Eusebius and Irenæus both agree that Linus was the second Bishop of Rome, into whose hands "the blessed apostles" Peter and Paul committed the church after building it, it could not have been at any other time than between A.D. 64 and 68; 3, that this interval of years happens during the reign of Nero, for Eusebius states that Linus held his office twelve years (Ecclesiastical History, book iii., c .13), entering upon it A.D. 69, one year after the death of Nero, and dying himself in 81. After that the author maintains, on very solid grounds, that Peter could not be in Rome A.D. 64, for he was then in Babylon; wherefrom he wrote his first Epistle, the date of which is fixed by Dr. Lardner and other critics at precisely this year. But we believe that his best argument is in proving that it was not in the character of the cowardly Peter to risk himself in such close neighborhood with Nero, who "was feeding the wild beasts of the Amphitheatre with the flesh and bones of Christians" at that time.

Perhaps the Church of Rome was but consistent in choosing as her titular founder the apostle who thrice denied his master at the moment of danger; and the only one, moreover, except Judas, who provoked Christ in such a way as to be addressed as the "Enemy." "Get thee behind me, SATAN!" exclaims Jesus, rebuking the taunting apostle.

There is a tradition in the Greek Church which has never found favor at the Vatican. The former traces its origin to one of the Gnostic leaders – Basilides, perhaps, who lived under Trajan and Adrian, at the end of the first and the beginning of the second century. With regard to this particular tradition, if the Gnostic is Basilides, then he must be accepted as a sufficient authority, having claimed to have been a disciple of the Apostle Matthew, and to have had for master Glaucias, a disciple of St. Peter himself. Were the narrative attributed to him authenticated, the London Committee for the Revision of the Bible would have to add a new verse to Matthew, Mark, and John, who tell the story of Peter's denial of Christ.

This tradition, then, of which we have been speaking, affirms that, when frightened at the accusation of the servant of the high priest, the apostle had thrice denied his master, and the cock had crowed, Jesus, who was then passing through the hall in custody of the soldiers, turned, and, looking at Peter, said: "Verily, I say unto thee, Peter, thou shalt deny me throughout the coming ages, and never stop until thou shalt be old, and shalt stretch forth thy hands, and another shall gird thee and carry thee wither thou wouldst not."

The latter part of this sentence, say the Greeks, relates to the Church of Rome, and prophesies her constant apostasy from Christ, under the mask of false religion. Later, it was inserted in the twenty-first chapter of John, but the whole of this chapter had been pronounced a forgery, even before it was found that this Gospel was never written by John the Apostle at all.

The anonymous author of **Supernatural Religion**, a work which in two years passed through several editions, and which is alleged to have been written by an eminent theologian, proves conclusively the spuriousness of the four gospels, or at least their complete transformation in the hands of the too-zealous Irenæus and his champions. The fourth gospel is completely upset by this able author; the extraordinary forgeries of the Fathers of the early centuries are plainly demonstrated, and the relative value of the synoptics is discussed with an unprecedented power of logic. The work carries conviction in its every line.

From it we quote the following: "We gain infinitely more than we lose in abandoning belief in the reality of Divine Revelation. Whilst we retain, pure and unimpaired, the treasure of Christian morality, we relinquish nothing but the debasing elements added to it by human superstition. We are no longer bound to believe a theology which outrages reason and moral sense. We are freed from base anthropomorphic views of God and His government of the Universe, and from Jewish Mythology we rise to higher conceptions of an infinitely wise and beneficent Being, hidden from our finite minds, it is true, in the impenetrable glory of Divinity, but whose laws of wondrous comprehensiveness and perfection we ever perceive in operation around us.... The argument so often employed by theologians, that Divine revelation is necessary for man, and that certain views contained in that revelation are required for our moral consciousness, is purely imaginary, and derived from the revelation which it seeks to maintain. The only thing absolutely necessary for man is TRUTH, and to that, and that alone, must our moral consciousness adapt itself."

We will consider farther in what light was regarded the Divine revelation of the Jewish Bible by the Gnostics, who yet believed in Christ in their own way, a far better and less blasphemous one than the Roman Catholic. The Fathers have forced on the believers in Christ a Bible, the laws prescribed in which he was the first to break; the teachings of which he utterly rejected; and for which crimes he was finally crucified. Of whatever else the Christian world can boast, it can hardly claim logic and consistency as its chief virtues.

The fact alone that Peter remained to the last an "apostle of the circumcision," speaks for itself. Whosoever else might have built the Church of Rome it was not Peter. If such were the case, the successors of this apostle would have to submit themselves to circumcision, if it were but for the sake of consistency, and to show that the claims of the popes are not utterly groundless, Dr. Inman asserts that report says that "in our Christian times popes have to be privately perfect," but we do not know whether it is carried to the extent of the Levitical Jewish law. The first fifteen Christian bishops of Jerusalem, commencing with James and including Judas, were all circumcised Jews.

In the Sepher Toldos Jeshu, a Hebrew manuscript of great antiquity, the version about Peter is different. Simon Peter, it says, was one of their own brethren, though he had somewhat departed from the laws, and the Jewish hatred and persecution of the apostle seems to have existed but in the fecund imagination of the fathers. The author speaks of him with great respect and fairness, calling him "a faithful servant of the living God," who passed his life in austerity and meditation, "living in Babylon at the summit of a tower," composing hymns, and preaching charity. He adds that Peter always recommended to the Christians not to molest the Jews, but as soon as he was dead, behold another preacher went to Rome and pretended that Simon Peter had altered the teachings of his master. He invented a burning hell and threatened every one with it; promised miracles, but worked none.

How much there is in the above of fiction and how much of truth, it is for others to decide; but it certainly bears more the evidence of sincerity and fact on its face, than the fables concocted by the fathers to answer their end.

We may the more readily credit this friendship between Peter and his late co-religionists as we find in Theodoret the following assertion: "The Nazarenes are Jews, honoring the ANOINTED (Jesus) as a just man and using the Evangel according to Peter." Peter was a Nazarene, according to the Talmud. He belonged to the sect of the later Nazarenes, which dissented from the followers of John the Baptist, and became a rival sect; and which -- as tradition goes -- was instituted by Jesus himself.

Saint Peter

Ancient Bible Allegedly Reveals
Jesus Was Not Crucified

A 1500-year-old bible has been found in Turkey. Discovered in 2000, the book that contains purportedly the *Gospel of Barnabas* has been transferred by the Turkish government to the Ethnography Museum of Ankara with a police escort. Barnabas was a disciple of Christ, and in the work, claims that Jesus was not crucified, instead it says he ascended to heaven alive and Judas Iscariot was crucified in his place. Furthermore, the 1500-year-old bible states that Jesus Christ was not the son of God, but simply a prophet who passed on the word of God.

According to a report for *The National Turk*, the bible and alleged *Gospel of Barnabas* was seized from smugglers in the Mediterranean area in 2000 and held in a Turkish courthouse until safe transfer to the museum could be arranged. Authorities charged the thieves with "smuggling antiquities, illegal excavations and the possession of explosives," they since been sent to trial, Turkish police testified in regards to the incredible age of the bible, claiming it could be as old as "2000 years."

The Vatican has made an official request to be granted access to the 1500-year-old bible, however the bible that is said to be worth $28 million is currently held by the Turkish government securely. The holy words are hand written in Syriac in luminous gold lettering on loosely bound together animal hides. Syriac is a dialect of Aramaic – the reported native language of Jesus Christ. Aramaic itself is a nearly dead language, rarely present in today's modern society. Aramaic is only spoken in a small village near Damascus.

According to the *Christian Post*, merely photocopies of the holy book's pages are being sold for a staggering $1.7 million. In addition to the age and impeccable construction of the bible, the contents of the holy book is what makes it so valuable. *The Gospel of Barnabas* is not included in the New Testament alongside Matthew, Mark, Luke and John.

Turkish culture and tourism minister Ertugrul Gunay said the book could be an authentic version of the Gospel, which was suppressed by the Christian Church for its strong parallels with the Islamic view of Jesus. He also said the Vatican had made an official request to see the scripture – a controversial text which Muslims claim is an addition to the original gospels of Mark, Matthew, Luke and John.

This work opposes the ideas proposed in the widely spread New Testament, and instead has noticeable similarities to the Muslim interpretation of Jesus. The Gospel treats Jesus as a human being and not a God. The Gospel of Barnabas rejects the ideas of the Holy Trinity and the Crucifixion and reveals that Jesus predicted the coming of the Prophet Muhammad.

In one version of the gospel, he is said to have told a priest: 'How shall the Messiah be called? Muhammad is his blessed name.' Due to this fact, many followers of Islam believe the original gospel work was repressed by the Vatican Library.

In another part of the book Jesus denied being the Messiah, claiming that he or she would be Ishmaelite, the term used for an Arab. Despite the interest in the newly re-discovered book, some believe it is a fake and only dates back to the 16th century. The oldest copies of the book date back to that time, and are written in Spanish and Italian.

Protestant pastor I.hsan Özbek said it was unlikely to be authentic. This is because St Barnabas lived in the first century and was one of the Apostles of Jesus, in contrast to this version which is said to come from the fifth or sixth century.

He told the *Today Zaman* newspaper: "The copy in Ankara might have been written by one of the followers of St Barnabas.

Since there is around 500 years in between St Barnabas and the writing of the Bible copy, Muslims may be disappointed to see that this copy does not include things they would like to see. It might have no relation with the content of the *Gospel of Barnabas*."

Theology professor Ömer Faruk Harman said a scientific scan of the bible may be the only way to reveal how old it really is.

The Worst Popes in History

THE history of the Catholic Church is full of incredible stories that speak to mankind of blessings, curses, and everything in between. Millions have found hope because of Christianity – but millions have also been slaughtered in the name of God.

Starting with St. Peter, the world has seen a total of 265 official popes. While many of the holy fathers have indeed shown themselves to be saintly men worthy of trust and respect, there are a few whose names must go down in the archives of infamy, because they chose to hold the things of the world above the things of God. Others, while not as blatantly wicked, simply made bad choices that adversely affected the people they were supposed to be saving.

The life stories of these popes now serve to illustrate the sinful side of human nature and remind us that even God's own representative can lose his way. Here are ten of those stories, revealing some of the most power-hungry, sexually immoral, and ungodly men that have ever held the papacy – the worst popes.

Pope Boniface VIII (c. 1235 – 1303)

Born to a minor noble family in Anagni, Italy, Benedetto Caetani became a successful student of canon law and later a member of the Roman Curia, eventually winning the position of cardinal priest in 1291. He was elected Pope Boniface VIII on December 24, 1294 after the pious yet incompetent Pope Celestine V abdicated (possibly due to Boniface's own insistence). One of his first decisions as pope was to sentence Celestine to prison in the Castle of Fumone, where the old man was mistreated and eventually died ten months later.

Pope Boniface VIII

Boniface quickly became one of the church's strongest advocates for papal supremacy in both spiritual and civil matters, involving himself in foreign affairs to no end. His desire for political domination, of course, did not sit well with many rulers of the day, such as Philip IV of France, whose policies of clerical taxation angered the pope and prompted a string of bulls culminating in the famous Unam Sanctam, which essentially claimed all civil and spiritual authority for the papacy.

Other famous clashes include Boniface's feud with the powerful Colonna family, which led to several of their towns being demolished – Palestrina, for example, was razed to the ground and 6,000 citizens were killed. In addition, Boniface aroused the anger of Dante Alighieri, whose portrayal of the pope in his Inferno is anything but kindly, since he places Boniface in the eighth circle of his imaginary hell.

Boniface never quite attained to the absolute power he craved. Not surprisingly, his insatiable ambition led directly to a brutal beating at the hands of those who refused to submit to him, and within a month of this incident he was dead.

Pope Leo X (1513– 1521)

Often associated with Martin Luther and the upheavals of the Protestant Reformation, Pope Leo X is also well-known for being one of the most lavish, uncontrollable spenders who ever headed the Christian church. A famous phrase attributed to Leo aptly illustrates his greatest priority: "Since God has given us the papacy, let us enjoy it." According to Alexandre Dumas, "Christianity assumed a pagan character" as Leo doggedly pursued worldly pleasures.

Born Giovanni di Lorenzo de Medici, Leo came from a powerful family and enjoyed early favors that helped him acquire the papal throne by the time he was 37. A patron of the arts, education, and charity, Leo certainly deserves to be recognized for elevating the church's status, but his preference for money and political advancement rapidly exhausted the treasury. So financially unstable did his position become that he was eventually forced to pawn off furniture, jewels, and statues from the palace, as well as borrow huge sums of money from creditors (who were ultimately ruined when he died).

Pope Leo X

In addition to living a life of splendor, Leo practiced nepotism, famously used the sale of indulgences to finance the reconstruction of St. Peter's Basilica, and was even accused of homosexuality. In fact, some sources hold that he died in bed while getting it on with a youth. That accusation may or may not be true, of course, but one thing is for sure: Leo certainly let his love of luxury get the best of him.

Pope Clement VI (1291 – 1352)

Pierre Roger, a Frenchman, was the fourth of the Avignon popes, and took the name Clement VI for his pontificate. He was not a particularly evil man; in fact, his efforts during the Black Plague did much to provide refuge for the Jews, who automatically became the scapegoats for the deadly breakout. Described as a fine gentleman, a prince, and a patron of the arts and learning, Clement lacked one important characteristic that is rightly expected of popes – saintliness.

By his own words, Clement was "a sinner among sinners." His love for expensive living quickly drained the savings of his frugal predecessor (Benedict XII), and Clement resorted to raising taxes and selling off bishoprics to finance his worldly pursuits.

Throw in a little nepotism to boot, and you've got yourself a pope who may very well have been a man of decent character, but who also used his powerful position for his own sexual adventures, cheerful pleasures, and overall celebration of the world's many vices.

Pope Urban II (ca. 1035 – 1099)

It's undeniable that Otho de Lagery, who became Pope Urban II in 1088, was a talented diplomat and successful leader, responsible for establishing the modern Roman Curia and supporting reforms of the clergy. What he is most often remembered for, however, is his unfortunate role in launching a bloody holy war against Muslims that has since come to be known as The First Crusade.

In 1095, Byzantine Emperor Alexios I requested Urban's aid in fighting off the Turks, who had conquered most of Anatolia. Urban responded favorably by

Pope Clement VI

using his remarkable rhetorical skills to preach "Just War" – a holy, God-ordained crusade to liberate the eastern churches and the Holy Land from Muslim rule. By appealing to Catholic anger over the rumored (and often unfairly trumped-up) atrocities committed by the invading Turks, and by guaranteeing remission of sins to those who would participate in the fight, Urban was able to organize a large-scale uprising of piously outraged soldiers of Christ.

The religiously-sanctioned First Crusade, while successful in defeating Muslim forces in Anatolia and the Holy Land, was very costly in terms of casualties. Not only was there a huge loss of lives on both sides, but the horrible offenses committed by enraged Christians against Jews, Muslims, and even members of the "schismatic" Eastern church will always be a bloody stain on the pages of church history.

Pope Julius III (1487 – 1555)

Born to a famous Roman jurist, Giovanni Maria Ciocchi del Monte was elected pope in 1550 as a compromise candidate, and chose the title Julius III. While his early career in the church shows that he was very capable and successful, his papacy is known for being extremely ineffective and undistinguished. For the most part, Julius withdrew to his palace and spent the majority of his time seeing to his own personal pleasures and keeping out of political affairs.

However, it was his relationship with a boy named Innocenzo that tarnished his name more than anything. Julius discovered Innocenzo as a young beggar in Parma before ascending to the pontificate, and he adopted him as his own nephew. When Julius became pope, he elevated Innocenzo to the status of cardinal-nephew and bestowed many gifts and benefices upon him. In fact, the relationship between Julius and Innocenzo showed signs of being much more intimate than normal family ties, and many reports indicate that Julius actually had an extended sexual affair with the young man.

Pope Julius III

Pope Stephen VI (? – 897)

Little is known about Pope Stephen VI's personal life and background, although he was a Roman and the son of a priest named John. The reason his name stands out in church history is because of his involvement in what is perhaps the most bizarre ecclesiastical trial of all time – the Cadaver Synod of January 897.

As the name reveals, this grotesque synod was convened to put a corpse on trial. Stephen ordered it for the sole purpose of passing judgment on the freshly-exhumed body of Formosus, who had held the papacy from 891-96. Due to activities in Bulgaria which compromised his duties as bishop of Porto, Formosus had been excommunicated by then-pope John VIII (872-882), but after John VIII's death he had reassumed his bishopric in Porto and was elected pope in 891.

Political interests regarding rightful claims to the throne of the Holy Roman Emperor resulted in animosities that created a trickle-down effect and impacted later popes. Stephen VI and the Cadaver Synod are the most famous instance of reactions to Pope Formosus.

While it is not perfectly clear who exactly instigated the trial, the fact of the matter is that Stephen ordered Formosus's body to be disinterred and seated on a throne in the Basilica of St. John Lateran in Rome. A deacon stood next to it to act as its spokesman while Stephen lambasted it with accusations.

The corpse was condemned for transmigrating sees, committing perjury, and acting as bishop after being deposed. As punishment, his body was stripped of its vestments, the three fingers of the right hand used for benedictions were cut off, and all his former ordinations were declared null. The body was then buried, exhumed again, and finally thrown into the Tiber River.

Pope Stephen VI

Pope Sergius III (? – 911)

The son of a Roman noble and a member of the ultimately unsuccessful faction which opposed the policies of Pope Formosus, Sergius III must chiefly be understood through the biased writings of his enemies, since almost all sympathetic accounts have been destroyed.

Nevertheless, what we do have on Sergius suggests that he didn't quite measure up to Christian standards for piety. He was accused of ordering the murders of his predecessor Pope Leo V and Antipope Christopher in prison. It is said that his mistress was the young Marozia (later to become a powerful Roman noblewoman), and it was their son who became Pope John XI in 931.

The annals of the church of Rome tell about his life of open sin with Marozia who bore him several illegitimate children. He was described by Baronius as a "monster" and by Gregorovius as a "terrorizing criminal." Says a historian: "For seven years this man ... occupied the chair of St. Peter, while his concubine and her like mother held court with a pomp and voluptousness that recalled the worse days of the ancient empire."

This woman - Theodora - likened to Semiramis (because of her corrupt morals), along with Marozia, the Pope's concubine, "filled the papal chair with their paramours and bastard sons, and turned the Papal palace into a den of rob bers." The reign of Pope Sergius III began the period known as "the rule of the harlots"

It gets weirder, though. Pope Stephen VI's infamous Cadaver Synod had been declared void by succeeding popes, but when Sergius came to power, he voiced his displeasure with Formosus by annulling all of his recently reinstated ordinations. There is even a report that Sergius had the corpse of Formosus exhumed, tried, beheaded, and thrown into the Tiber – all over again!

After Pope Sergius died, the teenage son of Marozia - under the name of John XI - became Pope. *The Catholic Encyclopedia* says, "Some, taking Liutprand and the 'Liber Pontificalis' as their authority, assert that he was the natural son of Sergius III (a former Pope). Through the intrigues of his mother, who ruled at that time in Rome, he was raised to the Chair of Peter." But in quarreling with some of his mother's enemies, he was beaten and put into jail where he died from poisoning.

Pope Sergius III

In 955, the grandson of Marozia at the age of 18 became Pope under the name of John XII. ***The Catholic Encyclopedia*** describes him as "a coarse, immoral man, whose life was such that the Lateran was spoken of as a brothel, and the moral corruption in Rome became the subject of general odium.

On November 6 a synod composed of fifty Italian bishops was convened in St.Peter's; John was accused of sacrilege, simony, perjury, murder, adultery, and incest, and was summoned in writing to defend himself. Refusing to recognize the synod, John pronounced sentence of excommunication against all participators in the assembly, should they elect in his stead another Pope. John XII took bloody vengeance on the leaders of the opposite party, Cardinal-Deacon John had his right hand struck off, Bishop Otgar of Speyer was scourged, a high palatine official lost nose and ears.

John died on 14 May, 964, eight days after he had been, according to rumor, stricken by paralysis in the act of adultery."

Pope Sixtus IV (1471-1484)

Authorized the Spanish Inquisition and all its various forms of torture to gently convince the Jews, Moors, and Heretics that Catholic love and compassion were the way to God. While all this was going on it was rumored that Pope Sixtus IV was busy fathering children with his eldest sister and carrying on several bisexual relationships. Not surprisingly he was also said to have suffered from syphilis.

In addition to his complete lack of morality, and decency, there is strong evidence to indicate Sixtus IV was an avowed old-school Satanist in worship of Cybele as Queen of Heaven.

His obsession in resurrecting the Cybele cult to its former glory saw Pope Sixtus IV draft a new vision based on the piles of expensive rubble which Pope Nicholas V had created by tearing down the last of the ancient Roman civic buildings and temple ruins and carting it to outside the walls of the Vatican Palace. Using the now lost blueprints of Nicholas, Sixtus modified the design in line with his grand pagan temple to Cybele.

Pope Sixtus IV

In 1476 Pope Sixtus IV re-instituted an ancient Sadducee pagan feast in honor of Cybele, by nominating December 8th as the Feast Day of the Immaculate Conception of the Virgin Mary, Queen of Heaven.

Amongst the many historic stories of the vices of Sixtus IV, it is alleged he at one time drafted plans for the nunneries to become "brothels filled with the choicest prostitutes, lean with fasting, but full of lust."

Pope Benedict IX (c. 1012 – 1065/85)

Benedict IX, born Theophylactus of Tusculum, is known mainly for two things: 1) he held office on three separate occasions, and 2) he is the only pope who ever sold the papacy (to his own godfather, of all people).

Benedict became pontiff at a very young age, thanks to the political prowess of his father, who had managed to get the papacy reserved ahead of time for his son. Depending on what sources you believe Pope Benedict IX was given the papacy anywhere between eleven and twenty years of age. With little actual training or preparation that qualified him to act as pontiff, Benedict led a highly immoral life, and was accused of various rapes, adulteries, and murders. According to St. Peter Damian, Benedict was "a demon from hell in the disguise of a priest," and his carousing eventually caused him to be forcefully expelled from Rome.

Benedict managed to regain his throne, but then he was sidetracked by a prospective marriage (to his cousin) and sold the papal chair for a significant amount of money to his godfather, a priest who named himself Pope Gregory VI. His later repentance and attempt to resume his position created quite a controversy, forcing the German King Henry III to intervene. Benedict was subsequently excommunicated from the church.

"His life as a pope," wrote Pope Victor III, "was so vile, so foul, so execrable, that I shudder to think of it."

BENEDICTVS ·IX·PP· TVSCVLVM·

Pope Benedict IX

Pope John XII (c. 937 – 964)

Born in Rome, the young Octavianus practically had the papacy handed to him on a silver platter. His father, a patrician of Rome, made the Roman nobles swear an oath that at the next vacancy in the papal seat, Octavianus would be elected. Sure enough, when he was only 18 the reigning pope passed away, and Octavianus was chosen as the successor, taking the name Pope John XII.

Almost everything known about John XII is found in the writings of his enemies, so it's possible that the accounts we have are factually distorted. Nevertheless, the stories we do have are quite shocking – He was said to have been born to a fourteen year old mother, sired by a man who was both his father and grandfather. He apparently continued the family tradition by taking his mother as a lover as well as his niece and countless other adulteries. Apparently he turned the Vatican into a brothel, blinded his confessor, castrating and then murdering a subdeacon, invoking demons and foreign gods... the list goes on and on.

Even if some of the reports were falsified, it still appears that John XII made for a pretty bad pope. Rumor has it he was murdered at the age of twenty-seven when the husband of one of his mistresses walked in on them in bed and killed Pope John in a jealous rage.

Pope Alexander VI (1431 – 1503)

The reward for "Worst Pope Ever" arguably goes to Rodrigo Borgia, who enjoyed the benefits of having an uncle who just happened to be Pope Calixtus III. Thanks to his convenient social status, Borgia passed through the ranks of bishop, cardinal, and vice-chancellor, gaining enormous wealth along the way. In 1492, he was actually able to buy his way into the papacy, defeating two other opponents by means of bribery.

Alexander was so corrupt that his surname eventually became a byword representing the hellishly low papal standards of the time. He sired at least seven different illegitimate children by his mistresses, and didn't hesitate to reward them with handsome endowments at the church's expense. When low on finances, he either established new cardinals in return for payments, or he slammed wealthy people with completely fabricated charges, jailed or murdered them for said false charges, and then stole their money.

Not surprisingly, there is very little about Alexander VI that can be considered godly or even lawful. His goals were selfish and ambitious, and the orderly government he initially administered quickly deteriorated until the city of Rome was in a state of complete disrepair.

Pope Alexander VI

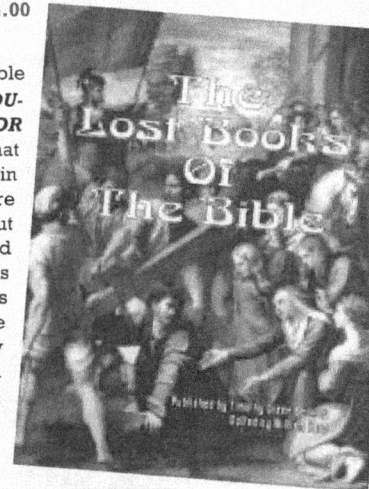

THE ARK OF THE COVENANT, AND OTHER SECRET WEAPONS OF THE ANCIENTS

Here is proof the ancients possessed "secret technology" that made them exceptional warriors. They might even have had the capability to annihilate their formidable foes utilizing nuclear-like devices. The question is how did they come about such an innovative science? Did they develop such devices on their own? Did God give the "chosen" unheralded power over their enemies? Or were ancient astronauts somehow involved? **David Medina**, along with **Sean Casteel, Tim Beckley, Olav Phillips, Brad Steiger** and **Tim R. Swartz** tackle an intriguing subject that gives evidence to the fact that the ancients had supernatural powers that were often lethal. For the first time, here is a detailed analysis of the mysterious *Ark of the Covenant*. Learn how the Ark was built and housed, and how the priests that tended it were required to wear protective clothing to shield them from what we call today nuclear energy. Moses even used the Ark to create a "controlled earthquake" to punish a rebellion by some of the Israelites. The desert ground opened up and swallowed the rebels. Also discover information on astounding air battles, and a very advanced type of "Thunderbolt Energy" that caused catastrophic disasters. There are also the issues of Magical Swords and superior aircraft mentioned in various ancient texts. This work contains fascinating insight into high-tech, death-dealing devices that predate our own by millennia.

8.5x11—Illustrated—ISBN-13: 978-1606111819—$19.95

SIGNS AND SYMBOLS OF THE SECOND COMING (Updated/Expanded Edition)

Author Sean Casteel maintains millions worldwide are awaiting the return of the Christ which could take place in our lifetime. Opinions on the Second Coming vary. "For example, there is a general consensus among a large group of UFO believers that we should await some form of open, mass landing of UFOs seen around the world. But, what if this expectation is not fulfilled until the Battle of Armageddon? Perhaps we are mistaken looking for a 'morally indifferent' landing on the White House lawn and should instead anticipate a vengeful mass landing in which the often seen flying saucers return to destroy the armies gathered by the Antichrist and establish the millennial reign of Jesus." The author speculates further as to the possible use of holograms to stage a "false flag" Second Coming and offers a checklist of signs and wonders to watch for in the countdown to the Day of the Lord.

8.5x11—104 pages—ISBN-13 978-1606111741
$14.95

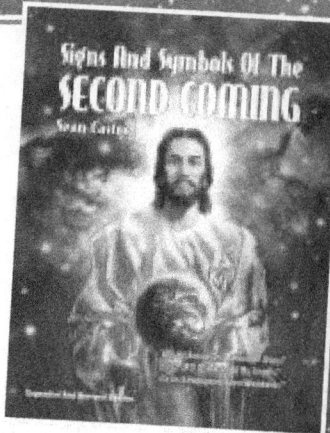

SCANDALS OF THE POPES, AND THE PROPHECIES OF SAINT MALACHI by Arthur Crockett.

There is more to the history of the Vatican than the public knows about, including the Scandals of Great Popes. Levitation and Teleportation of the Popes. The Mysterious Box No Pope Will Open. St. Malachi's Prophecy of the Popes. The Strange Story of Pope Joan. Pope Benedict XIV: Did He Write A Book On Miracles? The Vatican and Satanism. The Church's Obsession with Aliens. (Add $13 for related DVD)

8.5x11—ISBN-13: 978-1606111826—$14.95

SUPER SPECIAL: All 7 books listed on pages 4 and 5 just $105.00 + $12.00 S/H (U.S. only!)

Timothy Beckley · Box 753
New Brunswick, NJ 08903

THE CHARISMATIC, MARTYRED LIFE OF JOAN OF ARC—

by Sir Arthur Conan Doyle with an introduction by Sean Casteel. Warning! This is NOT an ordinary historical reference. Instead this work has been transmitted across time and space through a French medium as translated by the creator of Sherlock Holmes. It may be a book that Joan of Arc helped write herself. For how did mysterious disembodied voices lead a young French peasant girl to military leadership and victories in battle for her beloved France? This was definitely not written by the author — one of the most acclaimed spiritualist mediums of his time — by "ordinary means" — instead, it came directly "from spirit." It is an historical paranormal adventure that provides insight into a remarkable charismatic individual. .

8.5x11—188 pages—ISBN-13: 978-1606110782—$19.95